COACHING
BASKETBALL'S
COMBINATION
DEFENSES

COACHING BASKETBALL'S COMBINATION DEFENSES

Bob Abelsett

PARKER PUBLISHING COMPANY, INC.

WEST NYACK, NEW YORK

Library of Congress Cataloging in Publication Data
Abelsett, Bob
   Coaching basketball's combination defenses.

   Includes index.
   1. Basketball--Defense. 2. Basketball coaching.
I. Title.
GV888.A23   796.32'32   75-38511
ISBN 0-13-139220-4

DEDICATION

To the memory of the late Stewart Robertson, whose display of dedication to the game of basketball was unparalleled during his coaching tenure at Roseburg High School, Oregon. More importantly, Coach Robertson was a moral inspiration to all the players and coaches with whom he had contact.

How This Book
Will Help Your Defense

The natural evolution of defensive basketball from the basics of the man-to-man, through the zone era, and now into the modern phase of total pressure application has had a dynamic effect on the development of the game. By its very nature, defense has always been a counter force, an adjustment if you will, to the sophistication of the offense. This has never been more true than today. Today's defense is faced with a tremendous dual task: (1) stopping the multi-talented individual and the precision by which he operates within the offense and; (2) upsetting the movement of the complex continuity patterns so that its effectiveness is minimal. The conventional, or standard, defenses lack the necessary versatility and adaptability to neutralize these factors. *Coaching Basketball's Combination Defenses* offers the coach the opportunity to restore the "edge" to the defense. Defense, as we all know, is the backbone of any successful basketball system and it is here where our efforts pay the greatest dividends.

This book is written as a guide for the coach who desires to add some imaginative creativity to his defensive repertoire. Such is the concept of *dominating play without possession of the ball*–a totally unique aspect of basketball that is indeed revolutionary, and one which deserves added attention and exploration. Combination defensive systems enable teams to accomplish this even though they may not possess superior talent. With the increasing popularity of the combination style, the coach who fails fully to understand the potential explosiveness of this modern innovation will definitely find himself at a distinct disadvantage. Conversely, the coach who is willing and patient enough to commit himself to a working knowledge of the combinations will soon discover that he enjoys an added advantage over his opponent.

Coaches who plan to implement any or all of the combination tactics, as well as those that must counter these various combinations with an appropriate offense, will be able to compare their current system of defense with that offered in the succeeding chapters.

Molding a thorough defensive network centers around a single entity—flexibility: the ability to halt and control your opponent in two or more offensive phases simultaneously. The flexibility offered by both the pure combination defenses and their built-in matchup options virtually enables the defensive team to "attack and challenge" the team with the ball. This concept is clearly discussed in Chapters 2-6. Furthermore, combination utilization lends more power to your overall team dynamics by physically exploiting and mentally frustrating your opponent—from the players on the court to the rival coach on the bench.

This dedication to the combination defensive philosophy has acted as the keystone in the development of a positive basketball attitude at our school. There is, of course, no universal application for any defensive maneuver or technique, and each coach will add his individuality to any system, since he best knows his team personnel and the demands of his particular conference. During the years I have employed the combination system, it has proved to be both an effective equalizer during the "lean" years, and the stepping-stone to league championships in others.

Bob Abelsett

CONTENTS

COACHING
BASKETBALL'S
COMBINATION
DEFENSES

CHAPTER 1

Advantages of the
Combination Defenses

The straight zone, zone trap, match-up zones, pure man-to-man, and the sagging man-to-man defenses are slowly passing from us, although all are still invaluable in basketball today. From a coaching standpoint, the current cycle of the sagging man-to-man to the match-up zone phase is indirectly leading to the combination and the match-up combination varieties. If trends are followed, and there is supporting evidence that they will, the basis for team defense in the future will center around the combination defensive philosophy. The combination defenses we see today are not all evolutionary in nature. Many are innovative and born out of necessity; many, however, are also of the "cut and paste" variety. Whoever came up with the first combination defense is impossible to discover, nor is it a matter of importance for us to consider. What is significant at this juncture is a basic comprehension of the fundamentals concerning the operation of the numerous combination principles and their practical utilization in actual game situations.

Putting the argument very bluntly, the direct advantages of the combination defenses are that they, along with their match-up options, do a better job of *pressuring the ball, pressuring the better players, and disrupting normal offensive pattern flow* than any other defensive system. These three points are essentially what good team defense is all about! More specifically, the various features of the numerous combinations that bring about these advantages are that they: (1) are as adaptable and versatile as your team talent; (2) can force the offense to change its pre-planned tactics; (3) can keep a "marginal" team alive both in the conference standings and in attitude; and (4) are relatively simple to teach and incorporate into the total defensive team picture.

Throughout the history of high school and college basketball the defensive philosophies have been sound, yet simple, but have turned into chaos and reshuffling when confronted by the super team, the super player, or the power continuity offenses. I have felt for some years now that the transitions we, as coaches, have made in order to counter these situations could have been much more formidable and encompassing in scope. What we have done is to devise a defense to apply pressure directly on the ball and a totally different defense, when our aim has been to compensate for certain individuals or weak-side movement within a pattern. Furthermore, our defensive approaches have had only a single goal, when, in reality, we needed to design a system in order to fulfill several goals concurrently. Also, we have seldom sought the disruption of set pattern plays and the offensive flow of the attacking team. Thus, our defensive picture has been too narrow in scope to accomplish the completeness we seriously desired.

Since every team on the schedule does something different, offensive and defensive flexibility in the form of adaptation and versatility is perhaps the most important single element in any team sport. To cope successfully with the offensive variances, our defenses must possess both concepts. The day is gone when the team with the ball comes down the court and passes inside to the big man who puts up the shot, or passes back outside and screens for the guard or forward to shoot. Often, it was merely a two-or three-man game on offense and did not involve all five performers—one frequently wondered why the label "team sport" was tagged to basketball at all. With the advent of the zone and the sagging man-to-man defenses, the doom of those offenses was inevitable. Total offensive theory was radically revised to compensate for the shift in defensive tactics. This was not a change accomplished overnight by some of the country's coaching greats and handed down for us to follow; rather, the experiment was of the "grass roots" type, for we all faced unique situations in countering the deployment of the more modern defensive approaches.

Perplexing as the problem might have been, the offense regained its lost advantage with the introduction of the continuity patterns such as the Swing-and-Go and the Shuffle. No longer would a specific play be run for player A to shoot over a screen set by player B; and if that failed, return the ball out front and re-set the personnel and simply run it again until it produced a shot. The continuous offensive motion placed pressure on the defense from several areas at once, thus eliminating the obvious edge which the simple zones enjoyed for their brief period of glory. Movement, both with and away from the ball, presented new problems to the immobile and static defenses. The continuity offenses are still dominating play today as evidenced by the fact that today's teams possess more scoring power and reserve scoring potential than the game has hitherto known.

Defensive elasticity is a term we will hear more about in the near future as it is that entity of flexibility which implies that the *defense cannot be immobile*. Therefore, if it is to be a mobile force, it must also be readily adaptable in various ways and forms. Consequently, if the offense is a perpetual motion machine, the defense must do more than merely give the appearance of being a similar counter force. To engage the well-disciplined continuity team successfully, *the defense must be able to control the offense at its heart without giving ground should the ball be reversed or the pattern broken and a resulting free-lance move be made by an individual.* There is little question that the set zone system cannot lend itself to stopping this action. The man-to-man systems have a better opportunity to control this type of movement, but they, too, break down under pressure quickly and give up the high-percentage shot. Such facets of total defensive reaction are most significant and must be within your ability to control adequately.

Examine for a moment the continuity movement offered by the Shuffle offense in the following diagrams (1-1, 1-2 and 1-3). The Shuffle is, of course, primarily a perimeter offense offering quick scoring opportunities from the high angles and the corners and cannot be contained by any of the wide zones such as the 2-3 and the 1-3-1—considered by many as the best means of thwarting activity in these concentrated shooting areas. With continual movement being exerted by the offense, the standard zones cannot possibly hope to contain the individual talents of players 3, 4 and 5 on the initial strong-side maneuvers, once 3 has posted low. What becomes immediately obvious is the fact that the seams of the zone are readily vulnerable as the offensive rotation approaches completion. Added to this is the fact that the standard zone system is in no way capable of halting the penetrating passes to the inside cutters without weakening

18

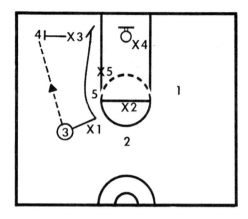

Diagram 1-1

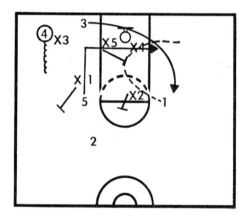

Diagram 1-2

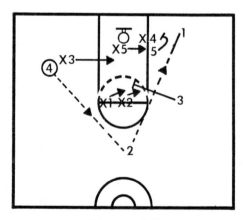

Diagram 1-3

the entire structure—passes from 4 to 3, 4 to 5 and from 4 to 5 to 3 are extremely difficult to stop. Note that if this particular Shuffle option is turned over and run from the opposite side without hesitation, it then forces the zone to shift and re-shift several times while watching for cutters penetrating both through the ball-side and the weak side, not to mention the players already stationed within the perimeter areas who all act as potential receivers when the ball is outside. Diagram 1-4 shows the foot patterns of the defensive post (X_5) with reference to his area of coverage. As the offense is rotated completely, he has made eight different defensive adjustments while attempting to watch for possible action—some direct and some blind-side—in his area of responsibility.

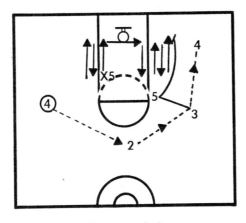

Diagram 1-4

Assuming that all five players on the court are those of exceptional talent, it is only natural for a team to accomplish a thorough job of defense with a tough, aggressive man-to-man. However, teams seldom get a stellar performance from each of their players at the defensive end of the court every night. Listed below are the three major elastic safeguards of the combinations which assure defensive stability. The following are set in motion simultaneously once the offense crosses mid-court:

1. The containment of the super-talented players of the opposition, while cutting pattern flow to a minimum.

2. Individually stopping a given number of the opposition's players upon command without changing the structure of the defense.

3. Clogging the penetrating passing lanes and also a majority of the non-penetrable lanes as desired. (Today, very few teams are hurt on defense by the clever dribbler, since his very asset is in direct conflict with continuity theory.)

These three points offer a great degree of security, which is a tremendous advantage in itself. Psychologically, there is little that will substitute for this feeling, at least from the coach's point of view. Coupled with this security is the necessary ability to switch the emphasis of pressure with relative ease. *The altering of pressure, both by degree and emphasis, on a team, as well as on an individual basis is essential as the game progresses.*

When using the combination defensive system, there are four significant points to consider regarding its total versatility. Each is a tactical approach and can be readily set in motion for a variety of purposes:

1. Applying pressure if behind and forced to come out and initiate action.

2. Being tied or ahead and exerting token pressure on a ball control team.

3. Presenting a totally confusing defensive network at the beginning of a game in hopes of thwarting the opposition's initial offensive thrust.

4. To bewilder a team at the conclusion of a quarter, half, or the end of the game, when the offense is looking to take the last high-percentage shot.

At one time or another, we have all found ourselves in a position where we needed to accomplish one of the above. In a majority of such situations, the transition from our original defense to the required adjustment was not smooth and often required an unnecessary time-out or needless foul to stop the clock to complete the adjustment. An underlying advantage of the combinations is that they are already doing this particular job and no drastic shift is required except to vary or revise the degree and emphasis of pressure exerted.

COMPARISONS WITH THE STANDARD DEFENSES

The major problems with the standard defenses is that they simply do not handle the talents of the super teams and exceptional players, nor can they effectively counter the continuity offenses. It does not take a talented player, or team, long to find where the strengths and weaknesses of the defense exist. Usually, two or three times down the court will spell out their attacking philosophy. Aside from a sound defensive system, the characteristics of the super basketball teams we are forced to stop are as follows:

— Height of a sufficient variety vested in more than one or two players.

— The ability to put points on the board quickly—scoring potential.

— One or more good percentage shooters.

— Inside rebounding strength and the ability to get the quick outlet pass and start the break.

— Power offensive patterns directed to the basket from a highly mobile continuity offense.

— The ability to control the ball and game tempo when the shooters are not hitting.

— A disciplined and confident attitude displayed by all members of the team and coaching staff.

This is not to say that the good teams possess all these traits. We can be thankful that this is not the case. Most of the better teams possess only a few of the characteristics mentioned above.

Usually, the contending teams in the leagues and conferences in which we participate have only one or two of the outstanding traits which make them dominant. Also, we must consider that these traits will be viewed differently by other teams because of the obvious talent matchups. Therefore, *it is imperative that we evaluate the opposition only in terms of the actual talent we can place on the floor at a given time to confront them.* This is where the thorough scouting report plays such a vital role in total game philosophy. Our particular defensive game plans are exclusively drawn from the scouting report—done by a member of the coaching staff who knows the true capabilities of our talent. The four sections noted below are the significant factors upon which we base the defenses for an opponent (the questions are fairly standard; however, when accompanied by the diagrams, they serve a most effective purpose):

1. Describe and diagram their offensive sets with special focus on their initial set.

2. Do they allow for an initial move either before, or to get into their pattern? Diagram.

3. From their offensive sets, diagram the foot patterns of their three best performers. Note any individual tendencies or team inclinations we might exploit.

4. How do they handle pressure when applied within their particular scoring zones? List the individuals who do not handle this, or who can be forced easily into error.

This is by no means the sole criteria for our entire defensive plan; rather it is for our goal defense and does not take into account back-court pressure variations. From our position, we have found that *the basis for a sound defense is neutralizing the opponent's strengths as early in the game as possible.* (More attention will be given this subject later in this chapter.)

As a coach facing a strong opponent with a less-talented ball club, one requires a versatile and adaptive defensive system which directly attacks the core of the opposition's strengths while effectively narrowing the offensive potential of the remaining performers. The coach is now forced to rely on the trap zones and the matchup series, or look to the combination style of defense for an equalizer. All three are obvious improvements over the standard man and zone defenses. Once the trap or matchup has taken place, it however, too, is just as vulnerable as the set zone since its flexibility is not sufficient to contain the offensive thrust of the truly well-balanced basketball team.

Unfortunately, there are no pattern formulas for stopping the teams having several of the earlier-mentioned "talents." It would indeed be most convenient if one could have a simple checklist of all the possible combinations that would be effective against any number of the talent qualities that make up the super teams. Space here is much too limited for such an exhaustive enumeration. However, each coach can easily categorize the qualities his opposition possesses and weigh the value of the defensive combinations against them. In the matter of game preparation, we all do this for every team on the schedule. What is important is that *you must be fully aware of how well your club executes the various combinations and matchup combinations before considering their use.* If it looks as if the standard triangle-and-two would totally inhibit all inside movement and individual efforts by team X on paper, this may not be the case at all for your team if you do not have the personnel to operate an effective triangle with two men low and two exterior man-to-man chasers. You can never expect much success from a defense you merely paste together for a temporary situation. Without careful planning and practice, the "cut and paste" defenses inevitably backfire into chaos and confusion.

DEFENDING THE 20-FOOT PERIMETER

There are two very basic, almost unchanging, factors concerning offensive thrust: (1) most shots taken by the offensive team result from either an individual move or a prescribed pattern play; and (2) 85 percent-90 percent of the shots by the offense are to be taken within 20 feet of the basket. For many high school teams, the perimeter will undoubtedly be lessened, possibly even scaled down to 15 feet in some instances.

If the latter of these points is kept in mind, the size of the floor that is most necessary to defend is greatly reduced in dimension—by more than 70 percent. For example, assume that we are dealing with a court 54 by 90—4860 square feet. Including the three-foot section behind the basket, a 20-foot perimeter would produce roughly 688 sq. feet of actual "high-percentage" scoring area. There is no question that this is a tremendous amount of territory to defend properly. However, in reality, all coaches realize that the true scoring power of their players is not equal—very few are good consistent scorers from the 18- to 20-foot range, especially when harassed by a defensive man with a hand in the shooter's face each time he has his hands on the basketball.

Since we feel that the main attacking area of the offensive team is that area within 20 feet of the basket, our defense is designed not to extend beyond this perimeter under normal circumstances. Once the offense consistently proves that it can score from outside the pre-established defensive perimeter arc, we will then extend the defense to challenge this, but not before such a threat has been clearly established. Diagram 1-5 clearly shows that, from an offensive standpoint, the 688 sq. feet of the arc is more than enough space in which to operate a continuity pattern—either man or zone. Going one step further, each defensive man must be accountable for approximately 137.6 sq. feet of court area within the arc. On a one-to-one basis, this vast area allows too much freedom for the offense.

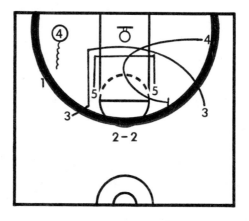

Diagram 1-5

In the following diagrams (1-6 through 1-10), note the coverage accorded the offense by several of the standard defensive alignments within the 20-foot perimeter. Keep in mind the previously mentioned principles contained in the description of the complete defense: pressure on the ball; pressure on the better offensive players; and disruption of the total offensive pattern.

What is most revealing upon examination of these diagrams is the fact that the offensive pattern continuity remains intact and never comes under any direct pressure. Given time, patience, and faith in their pattern, the team with the ball is lord and master of the game. Possession tends to dictate all terms and thwarts any serious challenge the static defense might mount merely by hitting the open man with a quick pass or opening a prescribed passing lane in either an attacking or retreating manner. There is little offensive adjustment that needs to

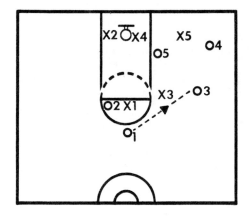

Diagram 1-6

Diagram 1-7

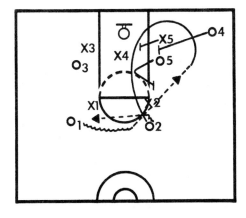

Diagram 1-8

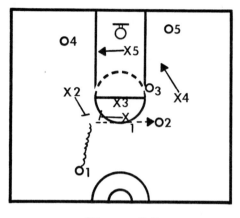

Diagram 1-9

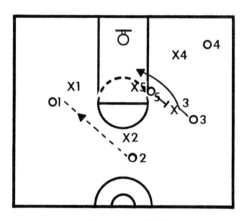

Diagram 1-10

be made by the opponent if the defense does not, or cannot, offer a substantive counter-attack. An open shot within the 20-foot perimeter is easily attainable by one or two passes, or a simple screen-and-cut move off the continuity. Unless the defense is able to upset the precision pattern execution of the offense, the typical 40-percent shooting team will soon improve its percentage by three to eight points during the course of the contest. This is only a natural occurrence since the offensive players will establish shooting confidence if they know that they can get their shots off with only token pressure applied. With each remaining possession their mental attitude will improve and they will become even more competitive.

Another glaring weakness visible in Diagrams 1-6 through 1-10 is that the offensive guards are reasonably open for good-percentage field goal attempts. In Diagrams 1-6, 1-7 and 1-9, the guard or swing-man becomes the single most viable member of the offense should he decide to attack the basket. If his first few field goal attempts are successful, his confidence will soar and he will be practically unstoppable. Regardless of the standard defense or multiple changing defenses employed, he is "free" to roam at will in the offensive flow with only token pressure as he comes in direct contact with the ball.

DEALING WITH THE SUPER PLAYER

There is no question that many of the players in the game today are multi-skilled performers and, therefore, constitute more of a threat to the defenses than those of the past. There are numerous reasons for this development, but suffice it to say that today's young players are handling, passing, and shooting the basketball with either hand at an increasingly early age. By the time a truly interested and talented boy enters high school, he usually possesses sufficient offensive skill to fit into the majority of continuity patterns. If he is one of those who seriously dedicates himself mentally and physically to the game, he might be fortunate enough to earn the label—superstar.

The super player can pick apart all of the standard defenses single-handedly, since he has acquired the skill, or simply has the instinct, to read them and react accordingly. Most highly offensive-minded coaches teach this "reading" concept as one of the preliminary steps to pattern execution. It is not surprising for today's player to bring the ball into front court and call a play that quickly isolates himself or a teammate for an easy shot at the basket. Whether the defense be man, zone, or match-up, the weak link or gap will soon be discovered by the players themselves through trial and error, or by the coach, and will be exploited to the fullest. The typical reaction to such an attack has been to mix the defense in hopes that this strategy might temporarily halt the offensive thrust. In a majority of the cases where this has happened, we were required to call a time-out to correct this situation. What a morale boost this is for the offense. They are fully aware that the game momentum has shifted their way—at least for the time being.

The superstar expects to be closely guarded by the opposing

team and as a result will be looking for the open man out of the pattern to assist for the easy shot, or possible lay-in. Gradually this will take some of the defensive pressure off him. He realizes that if he remains patient, he too will get his shots—it is merely a matter of time until a seam in the zone opens or a poor switch occurs on the man-to-man defense that will enable him once again to prove his shooting prowess. However, *the superstar, like the super team always has a vulnerable point or two which must be capitalized upon if he is to be held in check.* Finding this is, of course, the job of the coach scouting the opponent.

The superstar can be virtually nullified by many of the combination defenses. There are several means of accomplishing this without weakening your total defensive picture. The philosophies vary as to the degree and emphasis required. He can be prevented from getting the ball in front court. His movement within the continuity pattern can be reduced to a fraction of its full, or designed potential. Also, if he is a "spot" shooter, his favorite scoring areas can be thoroughly covered prior to his teammates' ability to get him the ball in these areas. Finally, he can be allowed the ball near his familiar shooting spots and suddenly find himself double-teamed and forced into a costly turnover. Whatever choice the combination-oriented defensive team wishes to employ, the superstar will be in for a long evening of continual and varied pressure—physically as well as mentally. Chapters 2 and 3 detail the methods of "denial" coverage.

In the event that there are two such power offensive performers attacking your zone or man defense, the conventional approach cannot stretch far enough to compensate for those standouts without sacrificing adequate coverage of the other members in the offensive pattern. It is both conceivable and possible that the set defense will deter the strength of the multi-talented teams for a time; however, this is only basing potential victory on the slim hope of "chance success" and this is not what one considers a "blue-chip" move. The combinations possess the ability to halt two or three super players effectively. This can be done on an individual basis and also on a total team basis as well without sacrificing stability. Chapters 4 and 5 clearly outline these principles.

Standard defenses do have their value and it is important to realize this fact before venturing into combination commitments. Perhaps their greatest asset is their ability to put pressure on the ball. Most coaches who utilize the straight zone or man sets concentrate on this point. For years this emphasis was rewarded, especially in the high schools and the small colleges where the defense came out quickly to stop the ball, or alter its direction, and thus forced an abundance of turnovers as offensive penetration was initiated. One might logically ask why this philosophy does not reap such results today. There is no concrete answer, since many fine coaches still find a good measure of success from this tactical approach.

The concept of applying pressure directly on the ball as it is brought into the front court attacking area has steadily declined for two very basic reasons. Today's player can spot a trap and react quickly to avoid it by driving to the opposite side of the court (Diagram 1-11), taking his man one-on-one to wherever he desires in order to begin the pattern; or drive directly into the heart of the trap and pass off as the full pressure of the trap is being applied. Regardless of the tactics employed, the standard one-and two-man zone fronts cannot stop the talented ballhandler. He possesses many more versatile offensive skills than those players of the past who merely dribbled up court and passed off to one of the big men and considered his job done. A second, and much more significant, reason for the decline of direct ball pressure is the extensive use of the continuity offenses. With this type pattern, once the ball is moved into front court, both the ball and the five players are constantly moving. Since there is extensive reliance upon the reversal action involved in continuity theory, it is extremely difficult to double-team or pressure the ball and contain the weak-side cutters coming off the blind screens.

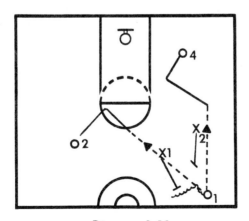

Diagram 1-11

FORCING THE INITIAL MOVE

To many a coach, myself included, it is of great importance —physically and psychologically—if he can cause the opposing coach to make a noticeable change in his style of play. We all have game plans implanted in our minds as to the initial course of action we want to pursue at the outset of the game. The majority of coaches like to prepare their players accordingly and carefully instruct them to run specific pre-set offensive patterns so as to see in what manner the defense will shift and what possible areas for exploitation exist. For us, this is the final phase of the scouting report and a true test of its validity. Some coaches are fortunate enough to rely on their talented players to find these openings and score quickly, thus building an early lead and taking away the defensive game plan of the opponent. Both schools of thought are fundamentally sound and are designed with a single point in mind—force the opposition into making a defensive adjustment early to combat the offensive thrust.

Once an adjustment is forced upon a team—whether it be offensive or defensive in nature—many possible consequences can be set in motion:

—A team not accustomed to adjusting can be forced into doing several things it has less confidence in, and thus find little or temporary success.

—If the adjustment is successful, the players may find new confidence in themselves and the coaching staff for making the "right move."

—If the adjustment is not successful, it could very well spell doom for the team for the remainder of the game and also have some post-game effects. This could range from the players to the "coaches" in the stands.

Depending upon the situation and numerous other factors, the initial adjustment is often the most crucial of the game. Regardless of the adjustment and its eventual outcome, for the moment, the team which forced the change in strategy (game tempo) definitely has the upper hand. The players on both teams know this and this in itself can be an extremely useful weapon if it can be capitalized upon. Most coaches will try to avoid calling a time-out at this juncture of the game because of its negative psychological implications. However, if the forced adjustment is of the variety that requires a time-out, the result is similar to that of a temporary coup d'état.

Altogether too often it is the offense which forces the change. On paper there is no question that they have the initial advantage since they know precisely what and where they will attack and all the players can observe the pre-set game plan become a reality. However, *it can just as easily be the defense that poses enough of a threat-factor to force the first major adjustment of the game.*

There is much to be said for the defensive system that is able to command a shift in the pre-established game tempo of the offense after the first few possessions. Even if moderately successful, the psychological edge is theirs. As coaches and players we have all experienced situations where we have come down the court with the ball and made the initial pass to begin the pattern only to find the pass stolen by a defender who has moved into the passing lane, or a cutter being denied his accustomed movement upon completion of the pass. The next time we attempt to run an offensive pattern play the situation reoccurs or something else happens to disrupt play. This is most frustrating from both the players' and coach's standpoint and immediately becomes a problem that needs a quick solution. For the psyche of his players and their confidence in him as their leader, the coach must be able to explain accurately what the defense is doing and how this must be countered. Even as he reaches a temporary solution, he is now faced with the dilemma of re-grouping his forces and restoring their confidence. All this early offensive adjustment during the first quarter, or first half, takes time and the score-board clock does not stop on its own to restore team solidarity.

The psychological side effects of a temporary offensive frustration mean more to a team than one of a defensive nature. Once you are stymied offensively, it usually takes considerable time in order once again to attack the basket properly. If the shots are still not there after the adjustment, or are just not going in because the players are not comfortable with the revised pattern, another adjustment is needed and so on.

The first three or four times the opposition puts the ball into play are significant enough to merit the use of a good matchup combination defense. This can often be only temporary but can also be the element that will throw them off-stride. If done correctly, you will hear the opposing players calling out "man-to-man," while others insist that it is a zone. This will all be done in a frenzy while the players are looking to the coach for direction. Suddenly there is temporary chaos in the offense since neither their pattern zone or man-to-man plays are resulting in the desired shots, nor are they even run properly because the passing and cutting lanes are always blocked. Many is the night we have forced the other team to call the first time-out and our players have come to the sideline grinning from ear to ear and saying, "Coach, they don't know what we're in out there . . . they're really upset, because they can't . . . ." This state of mind echoes confidence and is one of the foundations of great team defense and morale.

There is little need to disguise the combination within one of the more conventional zones at this point of the game. The objective you want is to convince all the players on the court that you possess a dynamic defensive weapon and are prepared to use it to the fullest to thwart the offense. Secondly, you want to see how far you can get with this type of combination and just how it will be attacked and by what personnel. Once this has been noted, you can revise the defensive techniques accordingly to meet the situation. The key here, as with any defense or offense, is not to stay with it too long—there is always a saturation point.

KEEPING THE MARGINAL TEAM ALIVE

The majority of basketball teams are marginal in composition. In the true sense of the word, marginal teams are those which possess 3-4 average ball players combined with 1 or 2 below-average players among their top six. Having been in situations of this sort for a couple of seasons, brought about a number of challenging problems whereby we simply struggled to keep the ball club alive in the face of over-powering odds. Primarily because of the totally unique manner in which our defensive system functioned, our teams were able to hold their own. There have been many times that, on paper, the opposition should have beaten us by 20 to 30 points because of their fine outside shooters or a tremendous amount of height and powerful inside game. Our utilization of the constantly shifting combination matchup defensive philosophy kept us in 95 percent of the games where we were "out-studded."

As you scan the opponent's starting five, plus early substitutes, in preparation for an upcoming game, one of the first items you note is how well your club can physically match up on a man basis. When you see such a variance as the following, you know that you must do something different to hold any hope for victory:

OPPONENT	HOME
Player 1. 5'11", playmaker and 40% shooter. A-minus student; good man def. player with 9.0 scoring ave. All-League (1st team)	*Player A.* 5'9",ballhandler and playmaker who shoots poorly. Plays decent defense because he is intelligent; 9.1 scoring ave.
Player 2. 6'3", fine shooter from outside and fair def. player. 10.4 scoring ave.	*Player B.* 6', fair scorer, 38% FGA and your best scorer. Basketball sense, but only fair def. player. 9.3 scoring ave.
Player 3. 6'5", sharp shooting forward from the outside. 8.6 scoring ave. Fair rebounder.	*Player C.* 6', sporadic off. player—9.0 scoring ave. Leaps well, but is horrible zone and man def. player.
Player 4. 6'6", post with fine inside moves and rugged on the boards. 12.4 scoring ave and 2nd team All-League.	*Player D.* 6'2", fair outside shooter. Good rebounder and plays sound man and zone defense. 8.1 scoring ave.
Player 5. 6'6", super player. Leaps well and is the leading scorer and rebounder. Operates effectively along the baseline. All-League 1st team, 15.2 ave.	*Player E.* 6'6", immobile and inexperienced post who was easily intimidated by the opposing big men in the league. Good rebounder, but too slow to make the proper moves on defense. 9.0 ave.

Height disadvantages at virtually all positions; potential scoring deficit of 13+ points on paper; scoring potential of first two key substitutes (11 for them and 4.5 for us).

The thought of having to play such a team four times in league play could have been most disheartening. Our players could clearly see how they were matched, or rather mismatched with the opposition.

However, they always felt they would be able to compete favorably and even pull off the upset. This proved to be true on several occasions and on those we lost, we were in the game until the final minute or two of play. The players realized that they were only "in" the game for the simple fact that their defense held strong.

During the several seasons that we were fortunate enough to possess two and three talented performers, the team attitude toward the multiple employment of combination defenses was also totally positive. Their talent, combined with their proficiency in playing the different combinations made them big winners.

SELLING THE COMBINATION SYSTEM

As in any new system you want to put into operation with your team, you must first have confidence in it yourself. The next step is to convey this feeling to your staff and then on to the players, managers, etc. Informal staff meetings, discussing the specific defensive needs of the team for the season might be sufficient to kindle an interest in several of the staff members. Quite naturally, the interest (at least the intensity of the interest) shown by the other coaches will depend upon the presentation of the head coach. The more thorough his initial presentation of the combination system, the better. Through experience, I have found that this should include several readings, a game film if available and an oral explantion of how this defensive structure would benefit the entire team. On the carefully selected staffs, there will be those who express a degree of reluctance and need to see the new system at work with the team personnel to truly measure its effectiveness. This attitude is invaluable, because it acts as a strong balancing force.

When the team defense section of the season practice plan is ready to install, it is imperative that the coaches and team observe a working model. Fortunately, early in the season this can be done without much preparation on the part of the players. One of the coaches can take the players aside to the chalk board for five minutes to explain what will be done defensively during the ensuing phase of the scrimmage. As a staff, we have introduced the varsity and junior varsity players to this defensive technique by several methods over the years and have found this means to be by far the most effective-

—especially when accompanied by a video-tape for all to evaluate at the conclusion of the practice session. After viewing the film or tape, both coaches and players have always expressed a strong desire to learn more about—or experiment with—this unique facet of team defense. This motivating factor has made for many a stimulating situation for both player and coach.

Once we approach this point in our total practice plan, we begin to describe the utilization factor of the various combinations on a team level—a *who, what, when,* and *where* concept. First, we describe the possibilities of using the combinations against league personnel and ask our players to match two or three such defenses to each of the teams in the conference. Each player is also to state the reason(s) for his selections. Given the opportunity to participate in the possible game plan choice, their interest in total team defense increases tremendously. Second, we size up our own personnel and practice the shifting of the various zone segments of the combinations in order that we can better evaluate which of the defenses we will be able to operate with maximum success. Complete shifting procedures are illustrated in Chapters 2-6.

Defense accounts for roughly 65 percent of our total team practice time. Because of this, we want the players to be continually aware of their defensive responsibilities. For game and also practices we have installed an incentive goal system. Note that all goals are on a team, rather than individual, basis, since it is the team that will reap the benefits of a strong defensive performance. A list of the goals includes:

1. Keeping the opposition below 1½ points per minute of play.
2. Holding the opposition shooting percentage below 40 percent.
3. Limiting the superstar to 6-10 points below his seasonal average.
4. Forcing 20 or more turnovers.
5. Winning the battle on our defensive boards by a 5 to 1 ratio.

Assuming we are successful in three or four of the established five goals, we should win the game or scrimmage. Since these statistics are kept during the practice sessions, it also makes playing defense much more competitive. Only one team plays the combination defenses in our scrimmage sessions and through close observation over the years, we have found that those players on the combination team psychologically feel that they will win. Consequently, all our players vie for berths on that team which enhances the intensity of our practices.

CHAPTER 2

Stopping the Superstar:
Box-and-One

Each year prior to the season opener, coaches throughout the country are pondering how to effectively stop the individual standouts they will face during the ensuing winter months. There is seldom a team that does not possess at least one very talented player. This individual can be the tremendously poised team and floor leader whose very presence on the court is in itself intimidating, or he might be an exceptionally proficient shooter from the outside, or perhaps a dominating force on the offensive backboards. Regardless of his specialty, he will be going full-tilt on the court and doing his utmost to shred the defense. Unless he is concentrated upon with a counter force and a great deal of specialization, he will fulfill his goal by leading his team to victory.

Although the super player can be somewhat slowed in his performance area, he will never be completely shut down over the course of an entire game. This is a most important concept for all coaches and players to be aware of and can never be overlooked. As coaches, we want our defensive players to respect the special skills of the specific individual involved and be prepared to limit his overall effectiveness. When setting up a defensive system, actual reality must always be placed in its proper perspective. *Stopping the star of the team is one thing, but stopping the entire team is another.*

As of now, there are two widely adopted single-coverage combination defenses in use throughout the country to combat a team's outstanding player: the Box-and-One and the Diamond-and-One. In their static (pure) sense, these combinations appear extremely vulnerable. However, once the various shifts and movements are enacted the defensive strength is multiplied considerably. It has also been said that they do not follow the old adage that a sound defense is a conservative counter force. This argument is no longer totally valid. The value of the single-coverage combinations is that they can offer the extensive coverage of the zone while also according the super player a tough and demanding man-to-man assignment.

To the untrained eye, or to young and inexperienced players, the true values of utilizing the single-coverage combination defenses may be most difficult to pin down. The direct and most visible effect of these defensive techniques is the manner in which the superstar is held down in the scoring column.

ADVANTAGES OFFERED BY THE BOX-AND-ONE

When describing the advantages of the Box-and-One, five major points are worthy of consideration:

1. The rebounding and area coverage rules remain virtually the same as the familiar "jug" or 1:2:2 zones—therefore, this combination is the easiest to teach as well as to learn.

2. This particular combination involves taking only a low-risk chance, since only one man is removed from the conventional zone set.

3. The Box-and-One is easily disguised within the framework of most commonly employed zones: 1:2:2, 2:1:2 and the 2:3.

4. This combination enables a team to concentrate on a particular individual with the assurance that the defensive man assigned single-coverage will always have "help," from his defensive team members, should the offensive star get momentarily free.

5. The Box provides for better corner and high-angle coverage.

The more one becomes familiar with the inner workings of this unique combination the better able he will be at evaluating the indirect effects of the total system. In the following paragraphs we will look at some of the practical approaches that make the Box-and-One such a viable force in today's game.

Both of the single-coverage defenses are dynamic and at the same time most unique. To some coaches, single-coverage defenses and their specific zone designation make a great deal of difference. They feel that if they are forced into single-coverage on a guard, only the Diamond-and-One is suitable since they believe they now need only one matching guard to counter the offense out front. The same school of thought uses the Box-and-One exclusively to cover the strong forward or center, since they believe that this leaves two guards out front to cover the offense's two guards, thus better thwarting their attacking efforts. Regardless of the philosophy chosen, there are numerous reasons for, and methods of, employing each of the single-coverage combinations. Perhaps this single entity is the true underlying beauty of the combination system of defense. When deciding whether to use the Box or Diamond, the coach must consider more than merely what floor position is vacated because of the single-coverage. Basically, there are three vital items that rank above floor position coverage in importance:

—Comparative rebounding strength of the teams.

—Inside or outside oriented pattern flow of the offense (penetration team vs. perimeter team).

—The ability of the defense to adjust within the total defensive system throughout the course of the entire game.

We are all aware of the tremendous importance rebounding plays in the game of basketball. Sound boardwork is one of the fundamentals of winning basketball. With this concept deeply entrenched in my mind, I have come to the conclusion that if our team is outmanned on the boards under normal conditions, we should think seriously about utilizing the Box-and-One as it affords the weaker rebounding team added strength under the basket. This is a point to note when examining the diagrams and situations outlined on the succeeding pages. With the exception of the shot taken from the corner, the Box retains the bigger men inside, thus increasing the chances for the rebound on the missed field goal attempt.

With reference to the second of the points mentioned above, most offensive patterns tend to penetrate inside as far as possible. This is good basketball as it is here that the high percentage shots are to be found. The team with a post attack, either high, low or, tandem, is somewhat easier to halt with the Box, primarily because there are more defensive personnel deployed in this area. *The middle of the Box is usually less vulnerable than the corresponding area of the Diamond.* Why? It is simply less square footage area to defend and your players are closer together, affording you a tighter defense.

The third argument noted is perhaps one of the most overlooked by coaches. However, it goes a long way to explain why the Box is more widely used today than the Diamond. The ease with which teams can shift in and out of the Box adds to its popularity. Teams can show a 1:2:2 straight zone and play it for two or three times down the court and then suddenly shift into the Box-and-One to deceive the offense for a short time. Once the Box-and-One has been detected, the defense can shift back to the straight 1:2:2 for a time and, if no single player is overpowering offensively, match up on the first cutter of their zone offensive pattern and fill the vacated spot in the zone (see Diagram 2-1). There are also numerous other means of employing the Box for purposes of confusion and deception which can be left to the imagination of the individual coach.

Analyzing Diagram 2-2, showing the set coverage of the Box-and-One with X_5 designated as the single-coverage or "denial" man on O_5 in each instance, will bring to fore several obvious points.[1] One of the direct effects readily observable from the diagram is that O_5 will undoubtedly discover that his total offensive possessions will be limited because of the body positioning of the defensive man. This becomes even more true when analyzing O_5's possible scoring possessions within the 20-foot perimeter arc. In most cases, O_5 will be a shooter of considerable talent and this is his primary value to the team. Once his total possessions are curtailed, his scoring potential is proportionately diminished. Again, we must realize that if O_5 is deserving of single-coverage, he is going to get his 20 points in the game. What we want to do is possibly keep him from setting the gym on fire with a 35-point night and hopefully keep him 8 to 10 points below his seasonal average. Ideally, he will become a different type of player when

---

[1]The term "denial" is most significant in our concept of teaching single-coverage defensive technique. It involves the total dedication in keeping the ball away from the superstar once he has crossed mid-court.

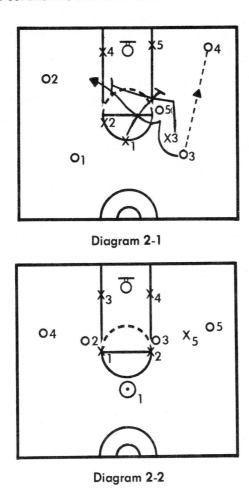

Diagram 2-1

Diagram 2-2

facing this combination since he will not be getting his accustomed pattern shots from the offense. This fact alone might be enough to upset his total game performance and consequently the performance of the entire team.

TRAINING AND CHOOSING THE "DENIAL" MEN

FOR SINGLE-COVERAGE

Proceeding on the assumption that the offensive star is a 50-percent-plus field goal shooter, we must note he needs 20 to 25 possessions per game in order to maintain his high scoring average. In a very direct manner, we inform our "denial" man that his primary task will be to limit his man to as few possessions in front court as reasonably possible without over-extending himself and the other members of the team. There are several means of accomplishing this objective, but, most coaches generally agree that this directive is most successfully carried out by blocking the pass-receiving lanes to the superstar (O_5) from his fellow teammates. Very seldom is one defensive man physically able to perform this demanding job adequately for more than six to eight minutes on the playing clock. There are two means of getting around this problem of fatigue, both in its physical and mental senses. Coaches today either platoon players who are assigned single-coverage, or plug these "denial" men back into the semi-zone and pull out others who best match up to test their defensive skills on the superstar for a short time.

We usually refer to X_5 as our chief "denial" man. X_5 could be a forward, guard or post and be assigned single-coverage accordingly. It is also possible for guards to be assigned forwards and forwards, post coverage, etc. In a majority of cases it makes little or no difference as to specific floor positioning. All our players drill long and hard on their single-coverage responsibilities and consider it the supreme honor to be accorded the challenge of stopping the offense's star player.

The major philosophy for this particular coverage concept is the standard man-to-man premise of "ball-you-man." Diagram 2-3 illustrates one of the fundamental drills used in teaching this technique to all the players in our system. This is perhaps the most basic of the drills we use. It is essential, however, in instructing our players, to strengthen their reaction speed in proportion to their peripheral vision so that they learn to pick up both the movement of the ball and also the position of a man constantly on the move. The drill also has a two-fold value in that it also teaches proper weight distribution and stance shifting with the relationship of the ball and the assigned man. Our "denial" men learn quickly just how close they can play single-coverage without jeopardizing themselves and the rest of the team. (For specific footwork rules see Diagram 2-4.)

Another drill we use to further emphasize this concept of "denial" defense on a slightly higher plane is to add another offensive player and declare him to be a permanent screener for O_5—Diagram 2-5. Now, X_5 must not only concentrate on the ball and his man, but

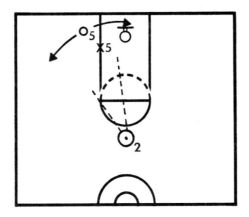

Diagram 2-3

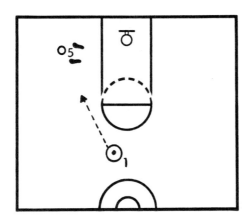

Diagram 2-4

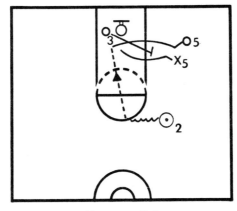

Diagram 2-5

constantly be alert for the possible blind-side pick. Since we do not allow any switching on our single-coverage defensive drills during the first weeks of practice, X_5 must learn how best to fight through the screens and be able to deflect or intercept the potential scoring pass from O_2 to O_5. During the early fall practices the defender is not allowed any verbal assistance on the screens, since we feel that his total position concept will improve if he is considering the constant possibility of the pick from the blind side. Once we are convinced our players are aware of the screening possibilities, we usually place one of his (X_5's) teammates on the baseline to call out the upcoming screens. The last phase of this particular drill series is especially valuable in building verbal cohesion—game rapport—between team members. *The "denial" man must be aware of all probable screens in order to do his job effectively.*

Our final single-coverage drill that is denial-oriented consists of expanding the drill outlined in Diagram 2-3. Here, we station four players around the 20' perimeter so that they are equally spaced and then attempt to work the ball to O_5 for a lay-in or good percentage shot. The same modifications can easily be adapted for the drill diagrammed in 2-5.

Assuming that the superstar is limited to 17 total possessions within the 20-foot arc, this factor alone does not necessarily imply that he will have a high-percentage shot at the basket. On the contrary, the defense is designed so that the star will always have a hand in his face when he decides to put up a shot at the basket. Even if he should slip away from the "denial" man, he will be picked up by the nearest man in the zone—only if he has the ball—until this "denial" man is able to recover and resume his defensive responsibility, thus releasing the zone man back into his normal defensive position. Limiting the highly talented player to three or four fewer possessions per game might just turn the tide for the marginal team on a given night. This obvious effect will force the offense to adjust significantly in order to offset the challenge presented by the defense.

As the game wears on into the first half, the chance that the super player will physically tire from the added pressure placed upon him by the defense increases. To be a superstar, he must be in excellent physical shape, but, there is little argument that any player drawing single-coverage will tire quicker than his teammates, since he must work much harder on offense yet still be accountable on defense. This significant fatigue-pressure factor is most important for the team employing the single-coverage to capitalize upon. Once it is noticeable that the superstar is reasonably drained (either physically or mentally) the defense can permit him ball possession near the 20-foot perimeter area and observe his shooting prowess with only token pressure applied. If a good job of "denial" defense has been done on O_5 throughout the half, it is highly unlikely that he will be overly effective from that range at this stage of the game. He may even feel more pressure from his own teammates and coaches to put the ball up more frequently and consequently "shoot his team right out of the game." This has happened more often than not when we have utilized the Box and also the Diamond. Because of this fact, we have made it a rule (but only somewhat standardized) for our single-coverage men to permit their man to handle, as well as shoot, the ball as often as he desires during the last two minutes of the first half unless, of course, he suddenly acquires the hot hand. During the second half of play, the amount of time and possessions O_5 is granted will be reduced or increased depending on the game situation and the physical condition of both the offensive and defensive players involved.

Furthermore, we realize that putting the "stud" through the paces against our single-coverage defense will occasionally exhaust the offensive performer, regardless of how much contact is applied. To make this player more mentally aware of our presence, we directly challenge him when it comes time for him to play defense. Attacking him on defense, or forcing him to switch and cover one of our stronger offensive players will definitely add to to his fatigue. Quite often the highly skilled offensive player has neglected his defensive fundamentals and proves vulnerable. Generally, it is an accepted principle to attack the opposition's most talented offensive player in anticipation of getting him into early foul trouble. The superstar is no threat if he is sitting on the bench plagued by fouls. Even if he should remain on the court, he will not be able to do the job demanded of him because the foul situation will negate his aggresiveness to a measurable degree.

As can be observed from the above, our goal in using the single-coverage defenses is to frustrate physically and exhaust the opponent's outstanding player and to upset his self-confidence —teamwise, as well as from an individual standpoint. Our coaches continually watch this player and his teammates, trying to discover at what point he reaches vulnerability. Once he has reached this condition he is virtually useless to the team and must be replaced by a substitute, or calmed down by a special time-out. As coaches we have had this happen to ourselves and seen it happen to the opposition on numerous occasions. When such an occurrence takes place during the game, our players are immediately aware of their efforts and seemingly gain a mental lift, thus becoming even more aggressive in their style of defensive play. This tenacity in protection of the goal is really what we are after when we utilize a special defensive technique.

For the better part of this section we have discussed the direct effects of the single-coverage system. Now, it is necessary to take a look at the other side of the coin. The unseen or intangible issues surrounding the single-coverage defenses (both for the Box and the Diamond) are two-fold:

1. The total strength of the remainder of the offensive unit will be tested to operate without its most potent performer.

2. As far as the offense is concerned, they must adjust their pattern execution in order to compensate for the loss of one of their members from the pattern flow.

Quite naturally it is these two indirect measurements of the combination style defenses that actually dictate the true course of the contest. As mentioned earlier in this chapter, one player, regardless of how great an individual star he may be, seldom has the distinction of making ''all the difference'' in the outcome of the game. There never has been one single individual who has done it ''all'' without the aid of his fellow teammates; at least not since Dr. Naismith tacked up the peach basket and made provisions for more than one player on a team.

We attempt to turn the opposing team's strongest offensive player into their weak link by practically nullifying his assets. If the talents of the superstar warranting single-coverage are genuinely that outstanding, his team is counting heavily upon him to pick them up offensively sooner or later in the game. Should the star find himself in early foul trouble and be forced to become less aggressive on offense, or totally forced—by the defense—out of the offensive picture, it then is up to the remaining four players to assume the responsibility for the scoring and offensive rebounding slack. In many cases, an individual-dependent team is totally unprepared for this situation. To them, this role is unprecedented and they are now asked to perform in a more skilled fashion offensively than they have been used to. Their reaction may be one of team unity in which they bind together and function as they never have before. Fortunately for the defense, however, this is not usually the case when the superstar has been weakened. What generally results is an Achilles'-heel effect. Added pressure and tension, uncertainty and unfamiliarity, pseudo-confidence from the coaches and fans, plus hesitation to take the offensive initiative usually prevent an individual-dominated team from "jelling" quickly.

For the single-coverage defense to be declared successful, it must force certain adjustments—on-floor coaching adjustments—in the offensive pattern flow. If the offense is to continue to look to the talents of its outstanding performer, newer and more frequent screens must be designed and set in order to free him for his quota of field goal attempts. Seeing that good picks are set and utilized in the proper fashion takes hours of practice. This, the one-minute time-out or the half-time chalk-talk simply cannot accomplish. For the coach who must resort to altering his offensive pattern flow because of a definite lack of talent or confidence in the ability of his other players to carry out the job, numerous problems are possible—some insurmountable. Chief among these is the fact that the remaining players can, and often do, feel somewhat resentful that the coaching staff has so little confidence in their offensive skills. Once it becomes obvious that team morale has been noticeably affected by the single-coverage defense employed, it is merely a matter of maneuvering and varying the degrees of pressure that will give a team the ultimate in defensive stability.

The choice of the "denial" man is ultimately dictated by the physical and mental characteristics of the offensive superstar. There can never be any fixed requirements for "denial" men per se. Offensive skills and the means by which they are employed prevent any real absolutes in the way of rules from being established. The closest thing to an absolute guideline comes in the form of personal pride and desire to stop the efforts of the opposition's star player.

As previously noted, it is almost an impossibility for one defensive player to apply single-coverage pressure for an entire game. Therefore, as we prepare for a game in which we will be utilizing the Box-and-One or the Diamond-and-One as a basic segment of our defensive system for that night, we take the three or four players who match up best with the superstar aside for further instruction and practice. There are three major considerations to note when selecting the "denial" man:

1. Quickness—this is the major item we look for. This is not to be confused with speed, rather out-and-out movement for three to four steps in relation to the man he will be assigned. Quickness enables one to gain and maintain pressure by always being in position. Therefore, the player who is quick can intimidate, as well as intercept potential penetrating passes to the man he is guarding.

2. Anticipation—Since the superstar will be forced to run an individual pattern for most of the game he will be trying to rub his man off on a variety of screens to get free. Basketball savvy and/or a high degree of intelligence are the best qualifications that best fulfill this need.

3. Size—We attempt to match up as best we can on this point, but many is the time we have conceded five to six inches in height on our single-coverage match-ups if we are assured the upper hand in quickness and anticipation.

In order for the defensive player to anticipate offensive action, he must learn as much about the offensive player as possible. He must "go to school" and dedicate himself not only to the specific man, but also the pattern in which he operates. Certainly not all things that affect an individual's performance on the court are physcial in nature: psychological behavior has much to do with the game play of any player, or group of players. Prior to the film/video tape review sessions we give our potential "denial" men, we sit down with them in a classroom situation and discuss what general things seem to bother that player mentally while he is on the court. Once we come up with one or two items we feel we can capitalize on, we then decide just how, *in a sportsmanlike manner,* we can use this information to disrupt his court composure. There is never any place in the game of basketball, or any other competitive sport, for degrading, harassing, or taunting your opponent. This indeed is a ticklish matter and we tend to approach it with the utmost caution when instructing our players how to benefit from "psychological pressures."

Scouting reports and game films enable the players and a coach to evaluate many of the individual characteristics of the player we want to thwart. This is usually done in a special briefing session before practice begins early in the week. At the first showing of the film, the coach assigned to these players will have them focus their attention on the offensive individual only, and then they will discuss his overall performance and observable traits. Later that same day, the entire team will view the scouting report and the films and discuss the basic offensive and defensive tactics they most likely will face in the upcoming game. Usually on the following day, the "chosen few" will meet again with their assigned coach and go over a checklist concerning the player they will draw. The list includes the following:

OFFENSIVE PROFILE CHECKLIST

Player (name) _____ No. _____

1. Does he look for the opening and use it?
2. Percentage shooter or force shooter.
3. Tendency to favor move to right or left in setting up scoring moves.
4. Shot release—quick, average or slow.
5. Does he follow his shot for the rebound?
6. Use of screens:
   —sets man up well on screen with ball in his possession.
   —sets man up well on screens away from the ball
7. Are the majority of his field goal attempts taken from the pattern or from individual moves?
8. Passing skills—good, average or poor.
9. What is his usual method for getting open?
10. His major shooting areas:

11. How might he be psyched?

At this time, the coach will review the basic offensive patterns used by the opposition and discuss where and how the superstar receives the ball in the pattern flow. As this phase is completed, we feel that the potential "denial" defenders are reasonably prepared to cope with the offensive star.

There are two other points that deserve consideration when selecting a player for single-coverage defense. These include that the player be even-tempered, yet physical. He must expect to get pushed and bumped around in the course of covering his man and he must be able to give and take some of this punishment without loosing his poise. This is an essential point to dwell upon during the practice sessions as it will be rewarded during the actual game.

The final consideration in selection of the "denial" man is the role he is to play on offense. Ideally he is never to be one of the top two scorers. This player will have more than enough pressure on him to perform his defensive assignment. Many times it is simply not possible for another member of the team to handle the single-coverage, yet if one of the other starters is accorded "denial" responsibility, it gives him the feeling, and rightfully so, of making the team click. This is another of the intangible assets of such a defensive system—it assists in spreading out the glory in the game usually accorded the scorers and rebounders. Such an opportunity-based rationale is very important over the long season.

THE FRONTING, QUARTERING, AND HALVING DEGREES OF PRESSURE

Whenever any discussion of defensive positioning arises, the various degrees of pressure and body placement are near the top of the list. All the above are sound position techniques which permit the defender to gain a better position on his man in relation to the position of the ball. The fronting method simply requires that the defensive man station himself directly between the offensive man and the ball at all times. This coverage demands the ultimate in recovery-reaction speed and peripheral vision, plus the ability to fend off the blind pick. Quartering is applied in two distinct ways: the one-quarter body position which is seldom used unless we are encouraging that player to get the ball and; the three-quarter method which most of our "denial" men play throughout the game. Halving is merely what the term denotes —gaining half-body position on the offensive man in relation to the ball. (Note the various body positions of the defense as pictured in Diagrams 2-6 through 2-9.)

The position of denial pressure is dependent upon three variables:

—Proximity of the offensive man to the basket

—Proximity of the offensive man to the ball

—Game situation regarding single-coverage

each of which is subject to the specific individual assigned "denial" pressure. When used in conjunction with the Box, we seldom, if ever, use the one-quarter or halving technique since we desire to keep the total defensive network tight. Only if the ball is directly opposite the single-coverage area are our "denial" men required to open up this far. With the ball on the same side as the "denial" pressure, and single-coverage not on the post, we prefer our players to use the three-quarter method with their hands moving to close off the potential passing lanes. For all low-post "denial" efforts we always front, to discourage any penetrating passes inside. Since the Box is designed with two deep defenders, the "denial" man fronting the low-post will always have the security that one of the back-line men will be responsible for the high lob pass.

Fronting and the three-quarter technique of "denial" pressure are by far the most effective means for coping with the talents of the superstar. Both methods keep him out of the pattern flow and nullify him as a pass receiver. The major problem with each technique is over-committal by the "denial" man. When this occurs, one of the remaining members of the Box is obligated to pick up the star with the ball. Such situations were the pivotal reasoning behind using the combination defense in the first place and we naturally want to avoid them if at all possible. Another common problem with fronting and three-quartering tactics is that the "denial" men are more apt to be screened, thus forcing the other members of the Box to temporarily pick up the superstar or else leave him open until recovery can take place. Against the good teams there is no guarantee that this will not happen, therefore your players should be prepared for this recovery phase of defense as it will become important. Perhaps one of the great advantages of fronting and three-quartering the offensive star is that it

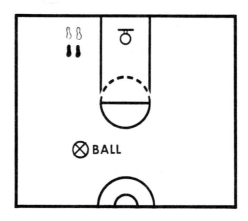

Diagram 2-6

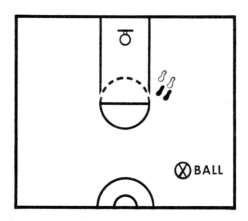

Diagram 2-7

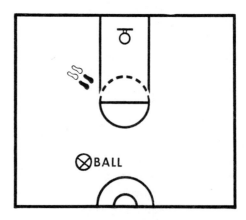

Diagram 2-8

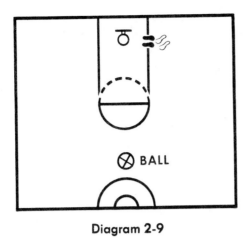

Diagram 2-9

enables the defense to use a smaller and oftentimes quicker player on their "denial" match-ups. With all the overplays, relative size makes less difference than in normal situations.

DECLARING FROM THE BOX

Once it has been decided to run the Box-and-One against an opponent, there are four basic rules/concepts which must be adhered to before any degree of success can hope to be achieved. These are varying in nature and must be clearly understood by *all* the defensive players. Included in this brief list are the following:

Rule 1.   Declare on the ball quickly without leaving holes in the Box.

Rule 2.   When there is not an offensive player in the assigned defensive area, that defensive man must sag toward the ball and to the middle to act as a plug.

Rule 3.   The entire defensive unit must have their hands up to deflect any passes at all times.

Rule 4.   All single-coverage players must constantly overplay all passing lanes and screen their respective men out as a shot is taken.

Rules 2 through 4 are virtually self-explanatory and we have already touched on some of these points earlier in this chapter. The greatest problem coaches have in running any of the combinations centers around proper declaration.

The decision to declare on the ball depends to a large extent on the position of the offensive personnel. With two offensive men out front (at the shoulders), the problem of where and upon whom to declare is increased. Because of the manner in which the offense is set and rotated, it becomes impossible for the coach to say that X_1 or X_2 always declares on the ball as it is brought into front court. Unfortunately, the solution is just not that clearcut. The lone exception to Rule 1 occurs when the single-coverage is directed to stop a guard. Here, the declaration need not be so quick as for "denial" coverage on a forward or post since the remaining guard does not usually pose as great an outside shooting threat.

To complicate matters on the declaration, most coaches will attempt to split the double front of the Box and also present an overload (strong) side to their offensive set. When this happens, X_1 and X_2 must draw an imaginary line between themselves extending from the top of the key to mid-court. The decision regarding who will declare rests on where the ball is in proportion to that line. Basically, there are two rules of thumb that can usually be applied when deciding which of the two defensive shoulder men (X_1 or X_2) will declare on the ball as it is brought into play:

—Declare on the side where single-coverage exists.

—Declare on the side opposite the overload if it does not involve the "denial" man.

Regardless of who makes the declaration on the ball it must be accomplished before the ball enters the 20-foot perimeter. Above all, this declaration must be thorough . . . completely halting the progress of the ball and forcing it to be passed to an outside receiver. This puts relatively no strain on the seams of the Box. However, if the declaration is not done correctly, one of the back-line defenders in the Box will be forced to pick up the first pass out too deep on the side, thus opening up several avenues for possible secondary penetration and easy scoring opportunities often result. Diagram 2-10 depicts the initial

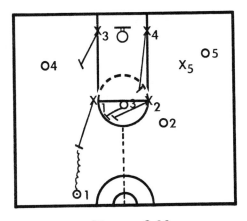

Diagram 2-10

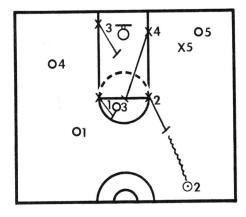

Diagram 2-11

declaration with an overload situation. Assuming that X_5 has single-coverage on O_5, X_1 must declare while X_2 and X_4 shift to fill the voids in the Box. The "decision to declare" on the weak side is quite naturally the simpler of the two, yet must be executed precisely. Once the ball enters the perimeter area, the players are instructed to force it to the outside and halt its progress there. The reasoning behind this maneuver is obvious as it then requires an additional shift by the offense to begin their pattern movement toward the basket area (Diagram 2-11).

SHIFTING PRINCIPLES

In all succeeding diagrams, O_5 will represent the superstar and X_5 the "denial" man.

Forward Coverage

Of the three offensive positions to cover, the forward is the most demanding assignment. Single-coverage responsibility remains the same, with emphasis on blocking the passing lanes, dogging the man through the intricate network of screens, and keeping him out of the pattern. Added to this is the fact that he must also be kept off the offensive boards: it is this dimension which makes his (as well as that of the entire team) assignment so difficult. The shifting movements of the other members of the Box are to be done in a much more peremptory manner. More attention must be focused on the inside game of the opponent. Seemingly, the major areas for concern are those situations where the ball is moved in and out of the corners. In all cases not directly involving O_5, X_5 must maintain a "ball-you-man" halving position with a step or two sag to the inside. Both back-line defenders, X_3 and X_4, along with the front-line defenders, X_1 and X_2, must constantly be alert to assume proper shifting responsibilities. Note the shift of both the front and back-line defenders as the ball is moved to the corners in Diagrams 2-12 through 2-14.

Diagram 2-12 shows the direct offensive thrust on the strongside. X_3 now must come out on the ball while X_4 assumes the void left by X_3, however, he can afford to play higher across the key as there is nobody in his coverage area. X_3 is instructed to open up on O_3, thereby cutting off the baseline and forcing him to the inside where he has help if O_3 should decide to make an individual move. The front-line (X_1 and X_2) shift is predicated upon what the back-line has already done to compensate for ball movement and position. In this particular instance, since X_4 has come high, X_1 can maintain his position but X_2 must quickly drop low and maintain tight inside position on O_4 for rebounding security.

In Diagram 2-13, O_2 has passed to O_3 in the corner. The basic shifting philosphy is the same for this as in the previous diagram with one exception. X_3 goes out on the ball, but X_4 must now come directly across the lane to guard O_4. If O_4 is an average or above average scorer,

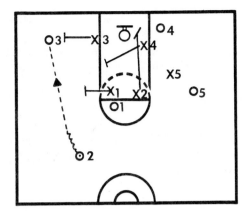

Diagram 2-12

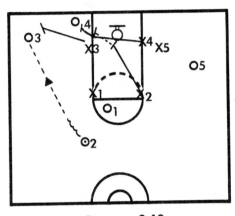

Diagram 2-13

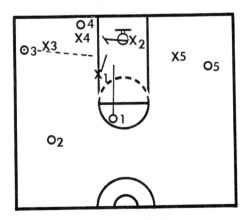

Diagram 2-14

X_4 will be required to front him and expect some back-line assistance from X_2 (shown by dotted line). Once again, X_2 is free to lend help in this case as there is nobody in his defensive area. The shift of the front-line away from the ball is, of course, dependent upon what X_4 is aiming to halt—pass or the shot. In any event, X_1 still has the responsibility for the possible penetrating pass from O_3 to O_1 breaking down the lane and attempting to split the seam of the Box zone. In almost all cases, X_1 will not contest the non-penetrating pass from O_3 back to O_2. *The Box cannot afford to gamble on picking off non-penetrating passes on the perimeter* since it then loses it ability to contract quickly.

Diagram 2-15 demonstrates the necessary movement as the ball moves out of the corner and back to the front. X_1 and X_2 might now have to come out quicker as one of the two offensive guards could be a good enough shooter to warrant this coverage. Given the hypothetical situation that O_4 is a good inside scorer, X_4 plays him to the inside and fronts or three-quarters him as the ball is moved around the outside. X_3 realizes that O_3 is not the strong forward and also shifts inside to prevent the ball from going into O_4 by closing him off, positioning himself so that he could return to O_3 quickly if needed.

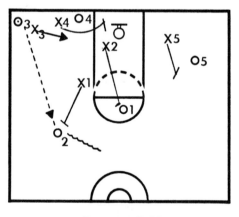

Diagram 2-15

Post Coverage

The task of defending the post within the confines of the Box is less difficult than defending either the forward or guard since he seldom roams out of the vicinity of the key area for his shots. The men assigned single-coverage on the post are consequently forced to front this individual as he is quite often operating low. In many cases, post single-coverage using the Box gives the appearance of a 2:1:2 zone, even the shifting principles are similar. Diagrams 2-16 and 2-17 demonstrate both the declarations and shifting techniques that are required for successful operation.

In Diagram 2-16, with the ball out front, single-coverage is on O_5 at the high post. With this overload situation to the left, X_2 must declare on the ball forcing the man with the ball to a position where help is immediately available. X_1 positions himself in a manner that favors O_2, but also in a possible "help" position if O_1 should drive past X_2. The back-line shift responsibilities involve gaining position on the men in their specific zone area respective of the ball position on the court.

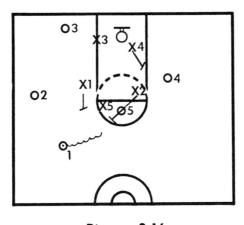

Diagram 2-16

Seldom do we ever cover the opposing post with our post. In a majority of cases we use our most physical forward for this "denial" coverage (providing he is not also our leading scorer) and keep our post inside. The reasoning for this type of coverage is relatively simple: (1) against the Box, the offensive post will receive very few passes inside because of the congestion factor presented by this defensive set; (2) a physical forward will usually be quicker, although possibly shorter in height, than the post and thus be able to gain proper positioning in order to thwart the possibility of all penetrating passes and; (3) leaving our post-man on the back-line of the Box affords us better rebounding strength on the defensive boards, since he must compete against forwards for the ball off the board.

Diagram 2-17 exemplifies coverage of the ball in the corner when a team is running a low-post offense. X_3 declares on the ball and X_4, seeing single-coverage in his specific area, attempts to gain rear position on O_5 as it is necessary that X_5 front him. X_1 will permit the pass back to O_2 but not to O_4 on the high-post or cutting down through the seam of the zone. X_2 has the responsibility for keeping O_1 off the boards and does this merely by dropping low to fill the space left by X_4. X_5 continues to front and three-quarter his man while he is within 12 feet of the basket. He can do this with little fear of getting burned by the high lob pass as there is built-in "help" from X_4.

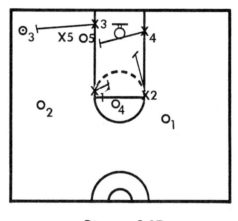

Diagram 2-17

Guard Coverage

Most guards that deserve single-coverage are outside shooters rather than penetrating ballhandlers. Therefore, the "denial" man in most cases can concentrate on his position in relation to the man and ball instead of worrying about getting beat on the drive to the basket. If he should get beat, the zone can easily collapse to halt this or expand to cover the man temporarily until recovery by the "denial" man takes place. The major problem the single-coverage man must counter here centers around the fact that he will have to deal with numerous screens to free the super guard for the open shot. Coverage on the guard can also be a bit more tenacious since the "denial" man does not have to face the situation of the high lob pass and the responsibility of keeping the man off the boards. We can often take the liberty of telling our "denial" men not to allow their man the ball once he crosses mid-court, unless he brings the ball up himself. This method of "denial" coverage is most effective, but it quickly exhausts your players and they must be rotated more often than forward or post "denial" pressure coverage.

The Box shifts are standard 1:2:2 shifts. Diagrams 2-18 and 2-19 show the proper positioning of the Box and "denial" as the ball is on the baseline and also at the top of the key.

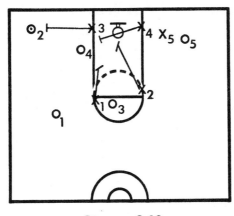

Diagram 2-18

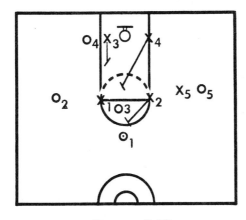

Diagram 2-19

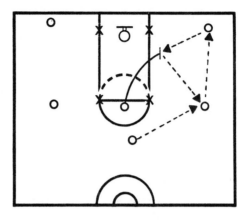

Diagram 2-20

A simple, yet thoroughly testing, drill we use constantly during the season makes sure our Box shifts are down correctly. This Box drill is constantly repeated, until the reactions of the players become machine-like. Diagram 2-20 notes the movement of the ball on this simplest of drills. Two minutes each day on the Box drill can avoid many costly game mistakes. The movement of the Box is as important, if not more so, as the movement of the "denial" man with regard to his body position technique.

CHAPTER 3

Stopping the Superstar:
Diamond-and-One

The second major dimension of direct single-coverage defense is the Diamond combination. In the minds of many coaches this four-man zone is considered to be merely an angular shift of the Box —either one man (position) to the right or left as deemed necessary. However, the Diamond is actually more involved than this. If one examines both its origin and identity, he will soon discern that the Diamond-and-One is a unique combination all its own. Because of the nature of its construction, the Diamond is the direct single-coverage counterpart to the Box-and-One. There are occasions when it is necessary to display both a two-man defensive front and also a one-man front. This is especially true if you are the type of defensive-minded coach who constantly desires to match the defensive set in accordance with the offensive set. This method of defensive theory probably includes the majority of coaches today. The ability to offer a one-man front with "denial" coverage on a specific individual is a must for the good defensive team.

Unquestionably, the Diamond-and-One is enjoying a type of renaissance. The increasing number of good perimeter shooters and perimeter continuity offensive patterns have made the Diamond a sound defensive weapon. For a number of years after its introduction, the Diamond combination lay dormant. The reason for this was justified for the most part. Foremost among the rationale was the rise in popularity of the inside-oriented, or post-dominated, game attacks combined with the fact that most teams seldom possessed more than one good perimeter (20-foot range) shooter. Seemingly, the Diamond got a stigma attached to it of being a rather porous zone, since the middle was open. Such discredit was unshakable for many years.

The vulnerability of the middle still exists to a degree. However, much new thought and innovative operational techniques have brought about a change in attitude toward increased utilization of the Diamond. Throughout the course of this chapter, we will attempt to discuss and evaluate the pros and cons of running this facet of the single-coverage system.

As one considers the possible uses of the Diamond, immediate comparisons with the Box arise. As a point of reference, a list of several contingencies relating to the decision of whether or not to employ the Diamond are noted below:

FAVORABLE

1. Covers more perimeter territory and consequently pressures the ball more effectively while it is on the perimeter. (see Diagram 3-1)

2. "Denial" coverage is made somewhat looser as the defensive perimeter of the four man zone has been extended. (see Diagram 3-2)

3. Offers a "natural" outlet to begin the break.

4. Covers the higher angles more thoroughly.

5. More unique and unusual in appearance, thus more confusing to the opposition.

NEGATIVE

1. Quicker and more mobile personnel are required to cover the expanded area.

2. The defensive middle of the zone is vulnerable to the good motion/passing team with a penetrating guard or forward.

3. Defensive rebounding is definitely weaker.

4. Corner and low-angle coverage is not as strong.

5. More difficult to learn and teach to players.

As indicated earlier in Chapter 2, the superstar is not the sole force that will make the total difference in the outcome of the contest; rather, it is the performance of the remaining four offensive players who are forced to pick up the slack as the single-coverage defense is applied. There-

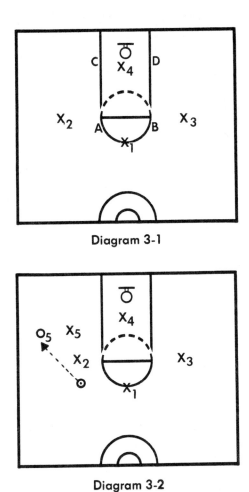

Diagram 3-1

Diagram 3-2

fore, it is these individuals who must be fully contained in order for the defense to key the team attack.

Concerning the "denial" coverage that is employed to complement the Diamond zone, only a slight modification is required. With the ball on the same side as the "denial" coverage, we still insist on the three-quarter method of man pressure, but can allow some halving pressure since the offensive perimeter is forced to extend itself in order to compensate for the wider defensive alignment. This is also true as the offensive players must take one more step or two to receive the ball than they do when working against the Box-and-One.

On the other hand, when the ball is opposite the "denial" man, we suggest that he play his man tighter than for the Box, as his offensive man will undoubtedly attempt to free himself to the middle of the zone. (Note coverage illustrated in Diagram 3-3.)

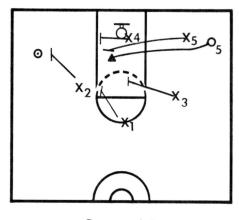

Diagram 3-3

Perhaps the most glaring comparative topic to consider with reference to the total defensive picture is that coverage which must be accorded the mid-section of the Diamond zone, as well as the corresponding rebound positioning. Command of this perplexing situation is vital to the success of any defense, but it, too, must be weighed in proper perspective with what the total defensive plan hopes to achieve. Naturally, the worst thing that the coaching staff can do is to overestimate their initial rebounding strength and sag-responsibility with regard to the middle. This is a common fear and one which all teams should go to extremes to prevent. For this reason alone, *it is recommended that the Diamond zone be employed only after defensive rebounding dominance has been achieved.* The multi-topical aspect of this part of pre-game planning warrants strong consideration, both on paper and during the early moments of the game.

There is a wide range of opinions centering around the use/function of the Diamond-and-One combination. Validity of each is, of course, dependent upon the individual coach and the capabilities of his personnel. In the following section, are two typical opinions with brief arguments attached regarding the utilization of the Diamond zone concept:

1. *Whom to assign single-coverage to?*

The Diamond is most useful when "denial" coverage is applied to a guard. Justification for this statement stems from the fact that since one guard (the better shooter of the two) will be single-covered, the defense need only present a one-man front to handle the activities of the remaining guard.

The Diamond is best suited for use when single-coverage is on either a forward or post. This premise is based upon the fact that the usually vulnerable middle can now be somewhat plugged by virtue of assigning "denial" coverage on a player who normally operates in that particular area.

2. *The idea of the one-man front:*

Such a defensive front is easier to split by the offense by merely putting two men in this area and forcing an immediate shifting situation for the four-man zone. Quick shifting can easily disrupt the defensive balance and pre-designed match-ups which the good teams try to maintain.

The single front zone makes for automatic declaration on the ball by the defense. Since there is only one player in this area, this avoids possible confusion regarding the initial declaration.

In most cases, this front matches up more frequently with the majority of today's zone offensive patterns which are themselves one-man frontal attacks, *e.g.*, the Shuffle, 1:4 and the 1:3:1, etc.

SITUATIONS FOR USING THE DIAMOND-AND-ONE

Numerous possibilities must be thoroughly explored prior to planning any defensive tactic. This is unquestionably true if one considers using the combinations—there are simply more factors at play. The decision to go with the Box or Diamond to complement the single-coverage rests entirely with the accuracy of the scouting report filed with the coaching staff. Naturally, more caution and attention must accompany the decision to use the Diamond since it is the more involved of the two. As with any defense, the coaching staff must constantly review and evaluate their most frequently employed defenses, plus those for use on special occasions with reference to both their strengths and weaknesses. Because the Diamond is usually inserted after the early rebounding pattern has been established, the above criteria are made even more significant. This preparation and confidence factor is a must.

As hinted at earlier in this chapter, the Diamond zone seemingly lends itself better to stopping the high-angle (30-60 degree area) shooting team because of its basic formation. For a majority of perimeter shooting teams, it is these high angles which provide the highest percentage of field goal attempts (see Diagram 3-4). Assuming this is the situation facing the coach who also must counter an All-Conference forward averaging over 25 points per contest, let us note some of the considerations he must thoroughly study before selecting his defensive game plan for the first half of play. The possible team characteristics could include any of the following:

Team # 1 —angle shooters, outside oriented and strong on the boards.

Team # 2 —angle shooters, outside oriented and poor on the boards.

Team # 3 —angle shooters, inside oriented and strong on the boards.

Team # 4 —angle shooters, inside oriented and weak on the boards.

Team # 5 —angle shooters, inside oriented and relatively even with us on the boards.

Team # 6 —angle shooters, outside oriented and even with us on the boards.

The circle indicates the selection by the coach of the items which he believes will most accurately apply in his choice of a defense—either a set zone, man-to-man, or combination—early in the game to counter the superstar and also establish a rebounding edge. Depending upon the success of this initial defense, one may implement the Diamond whenever he deems necessary or wait until the second half before using it. Of course, Team # 2 was the obvious model against which to use the Diamond. Proceeding one step further along this line of thought, consider the case if the opposition had been any of the remaining angle-shooting teams. Given the fact that the offensive superstar would

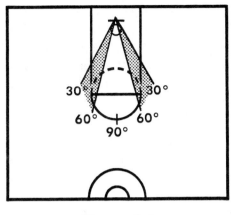

Diagram 3-4

receive single-coverage, examine the following possibilities facing the coach in deciding upon which defense would best benefit his team:

> Had Team # 1 been the opposition, the coach would have some reservations about using the Diamond until board/rebound dominance had been established. Because of the angle-shooters and perimeter offense he might well consider either going to, or remaining with the Box.

> Against Team # 3 there is little question that he would be better off with the Box, unless the angle-shooters began hitting consistently.

> Once the inside continuity was shut off against Team # 4, the Diamond could easily be put into practice and, if the other two assumptions are correct, should be successful.

> Against Team # 5, like Team # 3, the risk would indeed be high, but not entirely out of the realm of possibility; especially if one needed to take such a chance during the late stages of the ball game.

> Team # 6 could seemingly be adequately countered by a defensive maneuver like the Diamond. However, since "denial" coverage is on the high-scoring forward (who in all probability is also one of the leading team rebounders) the Diamond could prove effective very early in the game. This, naturally is also true for its use against Team # 2.

A further point to ponder, though not quite as significant as those mentioned above, is whether or not the opposition can make the quick transition from offense to defense. In other words, can you run on them from the rebound break or the interception with any measure of consistency? Depending upon what type of break philosophy is adopted, X_1, X_2 or X_3 could easily release for the outlet pass from the rebounder (Diagram 3-5). The methodology for each of these breaks will be accorded more specific attention later.

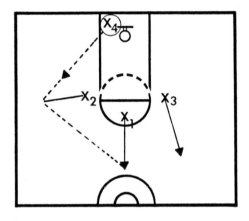

Diagram 3-5

The choice for the correct single-coverage combination defense must be based on an evaluation of all the above considerations. As can readily be observed, most angle-shooting teams can best be defended by the Diamond, as it continues to offer much stronger perimeter area coverage. On the other hand, the Box, because of its shifting rules and basic formation, lends itself better to stopping the corner-shooting teams. This need not always be the case as we noted in the examples cited. However, it is a good rule of thumb to follow, at least as a point of reference.

PERSONNEL PLACEMENT FOR DESIRED RESULTS

The Diamond formation adapts itself to any desired perimeter with little or no effort. In order to assure maximum inclusion with this defense, the actual positioning of team personnel is of the utmost importance. At first glance, the Diamond gives the appearance of a simple 1:3:1 zone without the middle defender. This is very close to being true with but two exceptions: (1) the baseline defender plays three to four feet nearer the free-throw line; and (2) wings are not generally as widely extended from the corners of the free-throw line. Basic positioning for the Diamond is as follows with regard to a 20-foot perimeter (see Diagram 3-6):

X_1 (Point)—roughly one step or so behind the top of the key, in direct line with the basket.

X_2 and X_3 (Wings)—two to three steps out from the right and left corners of the free-throw line extended.

X_4 (Base)—one or two steps, 3 to 5 feet, in front of the basket and in direct line with the goal.

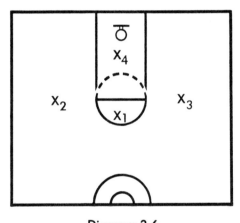

Diagram 3-6

Requirements for operating success when using the Diamond are reaction quickness and shifting intelligence of all players involved: *getting to the ball quickly without leaving gaps in the four-man zone which the opposition could exploit.* The players assigned the various positions must be able to act as a single unit with their reflex-action movements and shifts completely coordinated. Also, with reference to both the single-coverage assignment and the shooting/scoring pattern of the opposition, there should be two or even three strong rebounders inside.

All personnel assignments are relative because of the variance resulting from the single-coverage responsibilities. Therefore, there can be no absolutes in player alignment. Suffice it to say that the conventional placements suggest the following:

> Point—should be a "heady," quick, guard-type who can operate comfortably away from the basket. He must be able to make the necessary declarations once the ball is brought into the front court, and to force it out of pattern if possible. Since many coaches use this player as their outlet receiver for the break, he should also be a competent ballhandler and passer.

> Wings—must possess good lateral quickness as they have a large coverage area. Both wings will be required to rebound and, therefore, must be among the team's strongest board players. They will get a majority of the missed field goal attempts since the Diamond permits a certain amount of shots from the corners and lower angles which result in caroms to these particular areas.

> Base—preferably, he too should be a good physical rebounder. Depending upon the shifting technique adopted, he must also possess sufficient quickness to cover the lower angles on the overloads. He should also act as the team quarterback and call out the declarations and screens as they occur, since he has a majority of the plays taking place in front of him.

Diagram 3-7 clearly points out the areas of specific responsibility and also serves as a strong argument for the emphasis on lateral, as well as vertical, quickness of the wing position.

As noted earlier, the coverage positions in the Diamond will vary as to the single-coverage assignment. For example, if the single-coverage is directed against a guard, it can be assumed that the overall offensive movement will be measurably reduced in scope. Therefore, the Point is permitted to sag off somewhat as the major outside scoring threat is already well-covered. Consequently, the Wings will place more emphasis on interior movement and rebounding as more of the

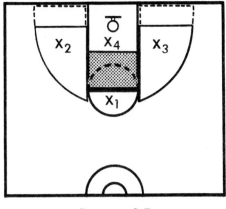

Diagram 3-7

scoring load will be focused on the play of the big men inside. Base positioning will be similar to that of the model since he must match up with the personnel in his specific area and flow with the ball.

Quite naturally, "denial" coverage on the forward necessitates different positioning and responsibilities. In all probability, the single-coverage on the team's outstanding forward could prompt both a reduction in total pattern play and also rebound potential. The Point will situate himself as in the diagram. Wing players will have less pressure on them to rebound and thus be better suited to apply greater pressure on the ball when it is in their area. In this example, the Base is forced to play somewhat lower than usual because of the amount of potential activity in his territory.

Existing single-coverage on the post causes a definite offensive rebound reduction, although the exterior pattern movement will usually increase to some degree in order to compensate for such a reduction. The Point must play his position as drawn in the diagram, but with considerably more pressure being applied both during and after the initial declaration has been made. Since the total pattern motion will be increased, the position of the Wings becomes one of reacting to halt exterior penetration. They may now play wider if the situation warrants such action. The Base is obligated to play a step or two higher—in front of the basket—as the major scoring threat is single-covered. He is freer to help his fellow teammates in chasing the ball.

SHIFTING RULES AND RESPONSIBILITIES

Shifting the Diamond is slightly more demanding than shifting the Box since there is the constant problem of the "open" middle that must receive attention. This factor alone makes the complete operation of the four-man zone much more complex than its single-coverage counterpart. Also, unlike the Box, the Diamond can be shifted in more than one effective manner—by the conventional method of involving the Base defender in the total shifting operation and also by accommodating the semi-mobile or totally immobile defender—often this is the big post man.

Under normal circumstances, the basic movements will be those of the 1:3:1 zone minus the middle defender. For both the Point and Base defenders this will remain true in most instances. However, they must be prepared to adjust their shifting pattern to compensate for the void in the interior of the zone. Since their vertical shifts will be those of a more demanding nature, there will be a greater area of lateral and semi-lateral territory for the Wings to cover. (Refer again to Diagram 3-7.)

Assuming that your club is plagued by an immobile big man, or a much needed offensive performer who is injured, or in foul trouble and only partially able to fulfill his defensive assignment, he can be "hidden" within the confines of the Diamond and played around. He should be assigned the Base position with the provision that he not go beyond a certain number of steps outside the key lane in either direction—this is usually restricted to one or two steps. Since his lateral responsibility is radically minimized, his vertical accountability must be increased to include more of the key area: perhaps the entire key lane, as high as the free-throw line. As this is accomplished, the Wings are now free to act as chasers in their coverage areas which will now extend from the baseline to the 60° angle line. The Point will then be forced to expand his lateral coverage responsibility and perhaps reduce the perimeter between the 60° angles both to the right and left of the goal. When "denial" pressure is applied to a guard this is generally a sound idea.

When using such a shifting sequence, the Base comes out of his area only when necessary for temporary coverage until a teammate can replace him. Once this action has taken place, he then resumes his assigned coverage area. This type of coverage places additional strain on the remaining members of the Diamond. Refer to the situation created by the overload in Diagram 3-8. As O_4 receives the pass from O_3, he is virtually open unless X_4 (Base) commits. X_3 immediately leaves his man and hedges to the ball, thus releasing X_4 back to the inside.

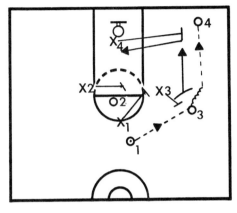

Diagram 3-8

As the ball is reversed back around the outside, the release action must be that of a quick chain reaction—one man adjusting to pick up the next and so on until the offensive reversal has been completed. This is only an emergency/extreme measure and one not recommended for extensive use even by a superior-conditioned team. This "Diamond-Release" concept is physically and mentally too punishing for most basketball teams and also tends to expose the weak link in the defensive framework.

The more conventional, or standard, shifting pattern of the Diamond is much less demanding than that described above, but it, too, requires much in the way of "help-side" sag away from the ball by all those involved in the zone. Also, with this method of shifting, the Diamond will continue to retain its shape once the prescribed movement has taken place if done correctly. This can serve as an important check as to whether or not the proper shifts have been enacted by all zone members.

An important factor is the ability of the players to shift quickly and correctly while getting to the ball and retaining the Diamond formation. This is, indeed, a difficult task for all teams regardless of the abundance of talent they may possess. Just getting to the ball from a wide spread zone formation is tough enough. Most coaches teach their players to "slide-step" to the ball as they approach, rather than crossing their feet to gain defensive position. The logic behind such technique was and still remains sound. However, the Diamond requires that the Wings and the Base cover vast amounts of territory as quickly as possible, thus foot movement of the zone defenders merits some attention.

We have used both methods for a number of years and have come to the conclusion that the "cross-step" technique has aided our players more in getting to the ball. Our total shifting reaction has been quicker and more effective. Many of the younger players still prefer to use the "slide-step" method as they approach the ball, but gradually adopt the "cross-step" in time. Those who have switched to the "cross-step" have suffered no noticeable side-effects when our combination shifts out of the Diamond into something else.

The pivotal argument against using the "cross-step" was that the defender would be completely out of position as he reached the offensive player and thus be at his mercy. This has not been the case when using this method with the Diamond, and only the Diamond, combination for three essential reasons: (1) the relative quickness by which the offensive man is attacked by the defender is, in itself, an overpowering act; (2) the rapidly approaching defender is protected by the semi-zone lying directly behind him and acting as a deterrent; and (3) the composition and effects of the "denial" coverage on the better player(s) usually prevents the zone defender from getting "burned" by one of the lesser talented offensive performers. Regardless of its unorthodox nature, the "cross-step" concept can be a helpful tool in improving defensive reaction speed.

In short, the more conventional aspects of operating the Diamond are easily mastered if the players have been fundamentally schooled in the sagging man-to-man and straight zone theories of team defense. Many of these elements and those which carry over can be readily observed from the following list of "rules" which apply to shifting the Diamond:

> 1. Force the ball to the outside at all times and keep it there until the zone is able to shift and halt the threat of damaging penetration.

2. Declare quickly and correctly on the ball as it is brought into the front court so that the initial shifts can be quickly implemented by all members of the four-man zone.

3. When an offensive player vacates a specific area, the nearest defender to that particular player must sag to the middle on the ball-side.

This list may seem too brief, but it is concise enough so that it remains clear in the minds of the players. Physically, they may not always be able to accomplish their task for one reason or another, but they will all know what they and their teammates should be doing concurrently. Simplicity is one of the game's most valuable intangibles.

It should be apparent that Rule # 1 is perhaps the most significant of the three since the mid-section of the Diamond zone is vulnerable to attack, especially if Rule # 3 is temporarily forgotten by one of the players. This, we all know, will happen occasionally. Because we attempt to force all movement to the outside when employing the Diamond, our zone defenders are instructed not to stop the dribbler completely as we do in the Box coverage, but rather gain defensive position on him and thus force the offensive momentum away from the middle. If this is only partially successful, our zone defenders will have sufficient time to enact the proper adjustments during this two-or three-second interval. Consequently, *all passing lanes leading away from the basket are actually open to encourage the offense to pass in a non-penetrating fashion.* These (negative-action) passes will seldom hurt any defense! What results from the majority of these non-attacking passes is that they merely consume valuable time and energy on the part of the offense. For any defensive-oriented team this is a definite plus!

Rule # 2 is also worthy of further note because regardless of what type of zone or combination defense is used, one is constantly faced with the perplexing problem of how and when to declare on the ball as it crosses the ten-second line. The initial declaration in any four or five-man zone defense is all-important as it is this adjustment that dictates the succeeding shifts of the remaining members of the defensive unit which must cope with all corresponding movement by the offense. This declaration also must be accomplished quickly with both confidence and knowledge. Quite naturally, confidence in this phase of the defensive attack comes only with knowledge and a great deal of team "talk" from the Base defender who directs the play as it unfolds before him.

In attacking the Diamond, most coaches will attempt to split the one-man front zone in an effort to confuse the initial declaration. Generally, the Point of the Diamond (X_1) will declare on the ball himself—refer to Diagrams 3-9 and 3-10—enabling the remaining defenders to shift into their respective coverage areas. This is by far the easiest approach. However, the more aggressive offensive coaches will go one step farther and also proceed to overload one of the sides, forcing one of the Wing defenders to makes the first declaration on the ball (Diagram 3-11). Whatever the offensive set, the decision to declare must be made without any hesitation and it must be correct. If not, the Diamond will crumble once the second pass has been completed, since the shifting rules are dependent upon correct execution of the declaration. Learning and repetition of the declaration principles from the Diamond will be time well spent in each and every practice session.

LOW-ANGLE AND CORNER COVERAGE

Since it was the Diamond rather than the Box that was selected as the zone basis to accompany the single-coverage assignment, one vital element that must be partially conceded is the fact that the offense will have more scoring opportunities from the lower angles and corners. Theoretically speaking, this is where the offensive weakness lies and thus is where the majority of shots are to be encouraged. With the various splits that will occur out front and the corresponding overloads on the sides, the Diamond will often be obligated to exert only token pressure on the ball in these specific areas.

Given the assumption that "denial" coverage in Diagram 3-12 exists on the offensive post (O_5), the corner and low-angle coverage in an overload situation becomes increasingly difficult. O_2 brings the ball into play on the weak-side of the court and the initial declaration rests with X_3, in a manner whereby O_2 is permitted to drive (in a restricted fashion) away from the overload. X_2 has followed Rule # 3 to the letter and adjusted to fill the middle void as the ball has crossed mid-court. X_1 also sags somewhat to prevent direct high-post action—giving up the non-penetrating pass to O_1 out front.

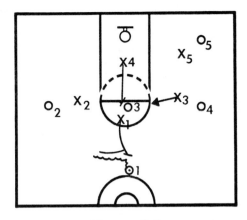

Diagram 3-9

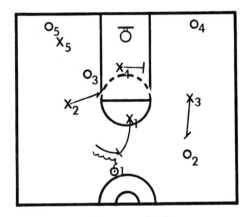

Diagram 3-10

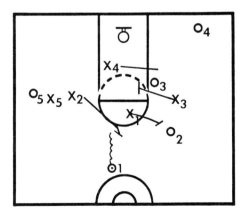

Diagram 3-11

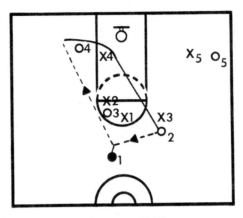

Diagram 3-12

In the succeeding diagram (3-13), 0_2 has completed the pass to 0_1 and cut to the strong-side corner. Once again, the shifts are according to the rules and X_4 comes out to confront 0_2, knowing that the ball will undoubtedly get to 0_2 while he (X_4) is still two or three steps away. However, he approaches 0_2 as quickly as he can and in a manner which will protect the baseline in the event 0_2 should attempt a drive in that direction. X_1 can slow the path of the ball by occupying 0_1 for as long as possible—without weakening the zone structure—before he releases the pass to 0_2. Note the completion of the shift and the attention accorded the remaining big man (0_4) inside.

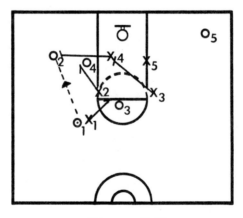

Diagram 3-13

For the simple reason that most teams will attack the Diamond combination by sending cutters through the zone, the Base (X_4) becomes accountable for picking up these players once they enter the key lane below the foul line. Diagram 3-14 illustrates the original zone responsibility of X_4 which is quickly assumed by the defensive Wing who follows Rule # 3—dropping ball side when there is nobody in his coverage area.

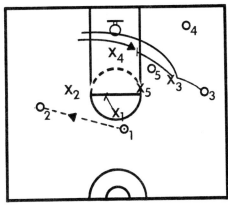

Diagram 3-14

POINTS FOR FURTHER CONSIDERATION

Seemingly, the major advantage offered by the single-coverage combination defenses such as the Box-and-One and the Diamond-and-One is that they allow for a more thorough accounting of two very distinctive elements: the individual superstar and the pattern continuity offense of the entire team. An adherence to the shifting rules for both the Box and Diamond zones enables the team to operate without sacrificing any segment of the defensive structure. In their design, these defenses are superimposed within and also outside the existing zone framework.

Two essential elements are fundamental when running the single-coverage, as well as those involving multiple-coverage, combinations—timing and execution. The offensive potential of the opposition must constantly be maintained in perspective. *You must be*

able to defend all moves that your opponent is capable of executing.
Also, knowing when to run a specific combination for maximum results takes hours of pondering over scouting reports and game films.
However, above all there is the fact that these various segments of the
combinations—SHIFTING, PERSONNEL, DECLARING, and
"DENIAL" COVERAGE—must be practiced daily with careful attention to detail and an aim toward perfection on game night. The rules
for the operation of both single-coverage combinations are simple, yet
thorough enough to be completely functional once the basic fundamentals of man-to-man and zone defenses are mastered.

CHAPTER 4

Applying Double-Coverage
Combination Defenses:
Triangle-and-Two

The multiple-coverage phase of defensive basketball stands atop the ladder as the most complete form of combination defensive theory. It combines the best of pressure man-to-man perimeter play with the interior security of the three-man zones. Both adaptability and versatility are exemplified by this unique defensive concept. There are numerous occasions during the course of the season when more than single-coverage defensive combination play is needed to stop, or off-set, an opponent who possesses more than one outstanding player. Surrounding this basic fundamental concept are a variety of reasons for employing double-coverage: (1) to present a virtual match-up whenever the offense has the ball in its front court; (2) as a ploy, early in the game, to force the offense out of their accustomed starting action; and (3) to nullify two similar or distinct segments of the opponent's individual strengths simultaneously.

The double-coverage combinations have the advantage over the single-coverage defenses in that they are better able to handle both the four and five-man offensive rotations. On the whole, many coaches are very reluctant to go beyond single-coverage combinations, even when faced by a team that shifts into a four-man pattern continuity, because they feel that the three-man zone will not be adequate in handling the remaining defensive responsibilities. This simply is not the case and throughout the course of this chapter we will attempt to present a direct challenge to this line of thinking.

Anyone who has experimented with any form, or forms, of the three-man (triangle) zone combinations knows that they are by far the most difficult and demanding of all defensive maneuvers to teach and employ correctly on a total team basis. There are more complexities in this defensive technique than in any other goal defense. As with all defenses, the practice time allotted for a thorough understanding of this system is indeed significant. In actual team hours, this is perhaps more true with the variations of the triangle than for any other defensive tactic.

A test of the total capacity of the triangle system of team defense is its rise in popularity, on all levels, during the past decade even though it is acknowledged as the most difficult to master. One can cite a number of reasons for this sudden acceptance, but, again, it would be impossible to place one reason or argument above another in importance. Most prominent among the arguments for its adoption as part of the total team defensive system are the following:

1. A variety of pressure emphasis is open to the defense.

2. Total continuity pattern disruption is virtually assured.

3. Allowance is made for built-in matchup play.

4. Continual rebounding stability is insured.

These are strong claims for any defense to make, let alone back up. Therefore, the reader is encouraged to let these points serve as a guideline as he reads this chapter.

DECISIONS ON WHAT PLAYERS GET "DENIAL" COVERAGE

A tremendous variety of elements enter into the final decision regarding which two offensive players are to receive "denial" coverage when utilizing a triangle as the zone basis for any of the defensive combination systems. There can be no absolute, or fixed, rules on who shall be single-covered, although it is strongly recommended that the opposition's highest scorer be one of the players receiving "denial"

attention. The remaining single-coverage assignment will be predicated upon the information gathered from the scouting report in accordance with the opponent's overall team characteristics. Choices for the
additional "denial" responsibility will usually include one of the four
players listed below:

—The second-best percentage shooter.

—Most aggressive offensive rebounder.

—Team quarterback (playmaker).

—Fast-break coordinator (outlet).

With minor exceptions, many coaches tend to believe that it makes
little difference which two players are single-covered. Coverage could
be placed on both guards, both forwards, post and guard, post and
forward, or guard and forward. Because of this variance in defensive
assignments and pressure emphasis, there is no question that this combination system is the ultimate in defensive flexibility and adaptability.

The "minor exceptions" noted above are worth a second
glance here, before moving into a detailed account of the operational
aspects of the triangle combinations. Simply because of the construction of the three-man zones, there are coaches who feel that their
defense is stronger if they limit "denial" coverage either to the two
perimeter players (preferably shooters) or one outside individual and
one inside power player. This, they claim, will give the defense a more
balanced appearance. Our staff has found this to be true for several
reasons. First, the three-man zone will be free to shift, "help," and
declare in a number of ways and operate more smoothly if there is less
interference and obstruction from the "denial" defenders constantly
moving through the triangle. There does not appear to be the added, or
built-in, back-up protection with the three-man zone as there is with
the four-man models and, therefore, they will not be able to extend-
and-recover as effectively. Secondly, if both the post and forward are
to receive single-coverage, the task of stopping the flow of the continuity pattern becomes increasingly more difficult. Also, when such
"denial" coverage is applied, the tightly knit three-man zones have
little effect on the opposition's outside game and cannot adequately
exert sufficient pressure on the ball. In essence, such coverage allows
the offense entirely too much freedom.

Regardless of the double-coverage selection, there must be at least one, and preferably two, of your top rebounders within the triangle zone. Whenever this defense is employed, it is imperative that rebounding dominance is assured—even more so than with the Diamond-and-One, since there are only three players who will be concerned with this vital aspect of the game. The lone exception or instance where there would be only one of the top rebounders within the triangle is when "denial" coverage on the post occurs. It thus becomes his ("denial" player) responsibility to screen out the offensive post whenever a shot at the goal is taken. If this is done correctly, the three-man zone should command defensive board dominance from the outset.

Throughout the past several seasons, we have found that our best results in using the triangle series were reaped when single-coverage was applied to the strongest inside scorer and the team playmaker, who usually played on the perimeter. This type of coverage forced more mobility out of the three-man zone, since they now were responsible for stopping the outside shooter. Although our personnel dictated such alignments, I am convinced that this is one of the most fundamentally sound means of employing this combination, because of its effect on the total offensive pattern flow. In most cases, the zone shifts were more than sufficient in handling the better outside shooters, while the three-man zone was virtually uncontested on the defensive boards.

THE STANDARD LOW-BASE SET

This is by far the most popular form taken by triangle combination advocates, primarily since it is the easiest to teach and its shifting rules are relatively simple. Its deceptive appearance and the manner in which it can be camouflaged within a variety of conventional defenses are reason enough for its intriguing appeal. With little, or no adjustment, most teams will totally confuse their opponent for a minimum of a quarter just by showing this combination early in the game. However, for this combination, like any defensive technique, to be successful on a tactical level, it needs to be employed at the proper time to really produce.

When selecting the standard low-base set, the size and shape of the three-man zone is an important consideration. In the western states, there are many coaches who insist upon maintaining an equilateral triangle at all times—all three defenders equally spread approximately 16 to 18 feet apart—depending upon the shooting skill of the opposition. Others prefer to keep both base defenders in relatively tight to the goal—not more than a step beyond the key lane to begin with—and having the Point pick up the ball (if not brought into play by one of the players receiving "denial" coverage) at the top of the key. It has always been our practice to keep the triangle reasonably tight during the early stages of the game and expand it in accordance with the demands brought about by the offensive attack.

The quickness and mobility of team personnel quite naturally dictate which method of triangle defense is most operative as do the shooting pattern and proficiency of the opposition. In either case, the Base defenders must be good physical rebounders who possess fairly quick lateral movement in the likely event they are forced to cover the corner when the offensive action tends to concentrate in that area of the court. The Point in the triangle series, as in the Diamond-and-One, must be a quick, guard-type, who is accustomed to defending the higher perimeter areas and also able to perform the proper declarations when necessary. Because of the area that must be defended and the limited number of players at a team's disposal to defend this expanse, it is a high-risk combination and thus requires "heady" ballplayers to get the job done in a satisfactory manner. Diagram 4-1 indicates the initial alignment with X_4 and X_5 designated "denial" defenders on the respective players.

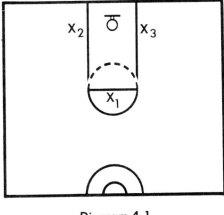

Diagram 4-1

Prior to putting the low-base triangle into actual game use, certain considerations should be observed:

1. The operational area of the three remaining offensive players must center from the free-throw line to the baseline.

2. Two of the remaining three players will be strong rebounders and, therefore, a continual threat to rebound dominance on the part of the defense.

3. Does the initial continuity pattern produce a shooting sequence of low-angle and corner shots? If so, can the triangle handle this and the long rebounds which usually accompany such a pattern?

4. Is this a team which consistently floods the zone areas by sending cutters to the lower angles?

5. What is the inside scoring potential of the opposition?

This version of the three-man zone is ideally suited, in either its pure form or as the result of a match-up for coping with a team having any one or more of the above characteristics. Naturally, the degree of success stemming from this defensive technique is entirely dependent upon the shifting and reaction capabilities of the triangle personnel.

THE INVERTED TRIANGLE SET

This unique approach to the triangle-and-two defensive combination system offers the appearance of an extremely radical approach to defensive play. However, adaptation in this manner further supports and illustrates the dynamic advancements made in the realm of defensive basketball during the last ten years. The inverted triangle can be a pre-planned (set) defensive maneuver or the result of a necessary team match-up to counter the offensive attacking style that constantly splits the Point once the standard low-base triangle zone has been detected. Many of those who have experimented with the conventional triangle zone are of the opinion that there is too much vulnerable territory in and around the free-throw line that is subject to attack. In a number of instances this appears to be so, since a majority of the power continuity offenses today have player movement in this area, and even if the triangle defense is not picked up by the opposing coach, he may successfully run his normal offense as long as it continues to generate a sufficient number of good shots within the higher angles of the established perimeter. Therefore, there should be some means of handling this problem while continuing to employ the double "denial" coverage concept with a back-up zone.

As with the low-base set, the actual perimeter of the inverted triangle is completely dependent upon the coverage it must accord the angles—in this case, the higher angles beyond the free-throw line extended. By and large, a majority of the triangle zone situations covered by using the inverted triangle will be smaller in area and perimeter than its low-base counterpart. Mathematically, this works out to approximately a 20-percent difference in perimeter and well over 28 percent in total area. When analyzed in relation to the other combinations, this is a statistic of measurable importance. Both team speed, in relation to the amount of actual court space that must be covered, and rebounding (the ability to get into proper position) are dependent upon area and perimeter sizes.

At first glance, when the triangle is inverted it closely resembles the Diamond-and-One without the Point defender. The lone Base defender will be in approximately the same position as the Base in the Diamond. Rebounding, lateral mobility, and the ability—or instinct —to "help" with the necessary declarations in the front-court are the standard requirements for all potential Base players. Since single-coverage is most frequently applied to one of the more consistent outside shooters, the two zone defenders playing the high angles should position themselves accordingly—perhaps one full step below the free-throw line extended and six to eight feet beyond the lane itself. Once again, quickness and rebound potential are the basic demands of this position (Diagram 4-2).

As a strong proponent of the inverted triangle zone formation, I have found that it is best suited for operation when:

1. "Denial" coverage centers on one or more offensive players who operate primarily in the lower areas of the court—below the free-throw line extended.

2. One or two of the three remaining players are fair-to-average outside shooters. If they are a serious threat to score from the higher angles, they warrant some attention.

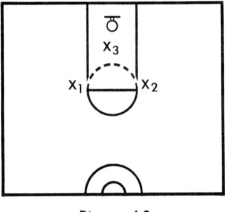

Diagram 4-2

3. We possess a definite rebounding edge over our opponent, or have one superior rebounder.
4. We are facing a perimeter-pattern team which strongly relies on the higher-angle shots out of their offense.

Total team rebounding appears to be noticeably weakened with only one player having permanence under the basket. This is simply not so! Combined with the practical philosophy of sending all members of the three-man zone to the boards is the fact that a greater degree of pressure can be applied by both the single-coverage defenders and also the high-angle defenders at the top of the inverted triangle. When this adjustment has been completed, it becomes difficult for the offense to take direct advantage of the situation under the basket with any real degree of effectiveness. Because of the above adjustment, this defensive set has provided many of our teams with some of the strongest rebounding outings we have had.

Since we have continued to send all three zone defenders to the boards, we have found it almost impossible to mount a wide-open fast-break attack. Therefore, we have been forced to go to a more controlled type of pattern break. Under normal circumstances, when running the low-base set, you are able to gamble and free the Point once in a while. However, this is much too complex and confusing when utilizing the inverted formation. We have also attempted to designate one of the high-angle players as the outlet man for the start of the break, but even this has been only moderately successful since he has been instructed that his main concern lies with the boards. Thus, our primary receiver for the outlet pass has been the better ballhandler of the two "denial" defenders. The obvious drawback to this is that he is seldom in a good position to get the outlet pass and initiate any threatening break action. He could be anywhere on the court and it may require two or three steps for him to get into position just to receive the first pass. Usually by this time, the opposition has made the transition from offense to defense.

SHIFTING AND OPERATION PRINCIPLES

The movement of the three-man zone is notably different from any of the combinations we have previously touched upon. Following zone principles, the zone set is predicated upon the position of the ball in relation to the single-coverage. Most zones point to the ball. The triangle combinations do this only when the ball is in possession of a player who is not individually accounted for. Therefore, *when one of the two players selected for "denial" coverage has the ball, the zone merely "hedges" toward the ball.* "Hedging" literally means to favor the ball side of a specific defensive area. This principle must be followed to the letter, since it will help plug the interior passing lanes near the goal. In Diagram 4-3, X₃ clearly demonstrates the use of the "hedge" technique as the ball is directly defended by one of the assigned "denial" players.

It matters little what the actual construction of the defense is, if

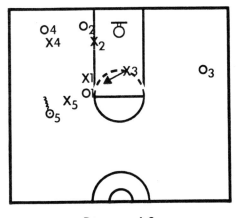

Diagram 4-3

it cannot shift and cover the obvious seams that exist in its construction. The purpose of almost all zone and combination zone shifts is to offer a matching defense to the offense. This can usually be accomplished by a step or two in a certain direction. Then, one asks, why is the shifting not always done correctly if it is seemingly so simple? Perhaps the answer lies in the total defensive picture the coach has drawn for his players. *All the zones and combinations that are being considered for use must have the same shifting base (rules) with only minor exceptions.* These exceptions must receive constant attention and reinforcement throughout the course of the season.

In essence, the operational rules for the three-man zones are noticeably consistent with those of the more conventional five-man zones. Shifting elements for the triangle(s) are as follows:

1. Movement of the three-man zone must be continually directed toward the ball in either a direct, or ''hedging'' fashion.

2. Never declare on the ball until back-up coverage is firmly established by the two remaining players.

3. The zone players should attempt to cut off all penetrating drives and passing lanes as the initial declaration takes place.

4. All zone players must ''slide-step'' when confronting/approaching the ball in their area. *The defender must always attack the offensive player with an open angle to the side where ''help'' exists.* Never open up to the side where the goal is!

5. The hands of the zone defenders should be chest high at all times and in constant motion, attempting to deflect any possible penetrating passes.

Shift when the declaration is made by the "denial" man

Whenever one of the assigned single-coverage players brings the ball across the ten-second line, the ''denial'' man must remain with him, attempting to force the ball to the outside and away from the strong-side set. An additional consideration we instill in our players is to be constantly aware of which hand the dribbler prefers to use and strive to take this away. In certain instances such action can upset the ballhandler (at least his confidence) and limit his effectiveness. This means of defensive attack is referred to as an automatic declaration and will not directly involve any members of the three-man zone. Diagram 4-4 illustrates the correct declaration and force play by X_4, as well as the "hedge" principle, involving the players in the low-base triangle.

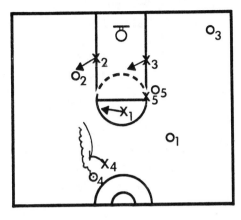

Diagram 4-4

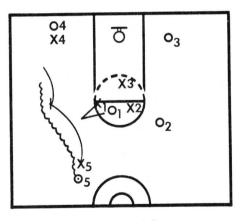

Diagram 4-5

The automatic or "denial" declaration from the inverted formation is quite similar. In Diagram 4-5, X_5 is unable to force the ball away from the strong side, but is successful in having the right-handed ballhandler use his weak hand and prevent him from making a deep penetrating drive. Should O_5 get half a step on his defensive man, the "hedging" done by X_1 and X_3 should be sufficient to discourage the furtherance of the drive. In 95 out of 100 cases, X_1 must avoid the temptation to come out and declare on the ball himself. There are such instances where the triangle members can switch and pick up one of the offensive players who has momentarily escaped the single-coverage, but very seldom is this procedure recommended for the initial declaration. The chances of the three-man zone being weakened are too great at this juncture for such a high-risk move.

Shift when the declaration is made by a zone member

Because of the strong pressure of the "denial" defenders, it is more often than not the task of one of the remaining three offensive players to bring the ball across mid-court and begin the offensive attack. When such a situation is encountered (see Diagram 4-6), the members of the low-base triangle must be prepared to react quickly and correctly. In this specific diagram, "denial" coverage is directed to the opposition's two guards. Therefore, O_3 is, in all probability, a forward who is a fair ballhandler, but not a strong enough scoring threat to warrant any further attention. Thus, the declaration will be performed as the ball enters the designated perimeter by the nearest member of the triangle and not before. This would be X_3, since player responsibility exists in the areas assigned to both X_1 and X_2. X_3's declaration is made smoothly and according to the rules set forth in the Diamond-and-One . . . "never attempt to stop the dribbler fully, but occupy him

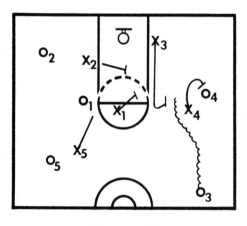

Diagram 4-6

sufficiently so that he is not able to penetrate the middle of the zone."
This gives the remaining zone players time to complete their shifts. As
a matter of record, most declarations from the low-base triangle are
quite simple since they are usually made by the Point.

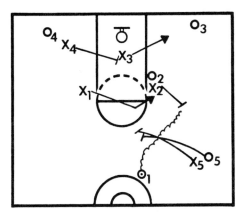

Diagram 4-7

The non-"denial" declaration from the inverted triangle, like
the others we have mentioned, appears relatively uncomplicated at first
glance. However, the decision to declare bears careful attention and a
considerable amount of practice in order to be effective. Diagram 4-7
is intended to clarify one of the frequently employed tactics used on the
perimeter when putting the ball into play—the crossing pattern. This
serves little practical function, but can somewhat confuse the declaration if the basic area rules regarding this move are not carefully observed by all members of the specific triangle zone. Here, the offense
desires to force X_1 to declare on the ball as the overload exists on that
particular side of the court. If X_1 were to make the declaration, the
effectiveness of the triangle would be greatly curtailed and suddenly
vulnerable to exploitation. The correct declaration in this diagram involves X_2 moving out to the ball as it enters his realm of responsibility
and cutting off penetration within the prescribed perimeter. X_1 should
slide across the key lane with the ball according to the shifting rules
and pick up O_2 while X_3 drops off to cover O_3. Both X_1 and X_3 must
attempt to gain three-quarter or half-position on the men in their areas.

Shifting against the overload situation

The overload is one of the most commonly applied forms of attacking the triangle, regardless of its shape (form). Perhaps the most frequently used overload tactic is the one directed at the base and lower angles. For our purposes here, we will stick to this premise. In Diagram 4-8, the ball is at the Point with the proper declaration having taken place and the corresponding overload thrust by the offense employed to free O_3 for a short shot from the low angle upon receiving a pass from O_2. From a tactical standpoint, it would seem to destroy the balance of the triangle if X_3 were to come across the lane and pickup O_3 as he receives the ball. The balance of the triangle and the off-side rebounding are now the responsibility of X_1, since it is he who must drop to the middle once X_3 has declared on the ball.

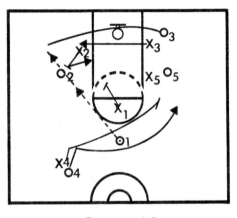

Diagram 4-8

Against the inverted set, the overload concept continues to attack the base area as this is obviously the most vulnerable point of the triangle. After the initial declaration has been made on the ball by X_2, Diagram 4-9 shows O_1 popping out of the designated perimeter, thus freeing himself temporarily from his defender (X_1) and prepared to receive a pass from O_2, who in turn cuts to the strong side. O_3 then attempts to set a pick for O_2 on X_3, thereby setting up an uncontested shot at the basket from relatively short range. X_3 has the play unfolding in front of him and cannot allow the screen to materialize. Conversely,

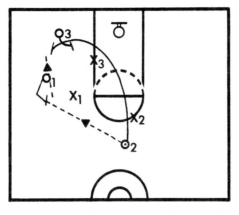

Diagram 4-9

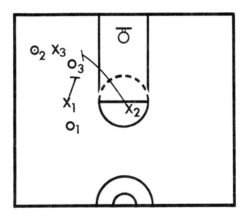

Diagram 4-10

he cannot get to the corner before the ball since O_1 could easily loft a high lob pass to O_3 under the goal before X_2 would be able to retreat sufficiently to prevent this method of attack. The completed shift is illustrated in the following diagram—4-10.

Many coaches are of the opinion that forcing a shift of this nature will create an advantageous mismatch underneath—whereby a taller O_3 would be paired against the forward-sized X_2. All things being equal, this would be true, but it is X_1's responsibility to help X_2 on the inside, making the penetrating pass from O_2 to O_3 virtually impossible to execute. Again, the passing lane to O_1 remains open, and since this is considered a non-penetrating maneuver, we instruct our players to give this pass up rather than the previously mentioned pass to the inside. O_1 was not considered to be an outstanding perimeter shooter in the information gathered by the scouting summaries and therefore does not pose the scoring threat that inside penetration would.

Corner coverage with the triangles

Covering the corners from the standard low-base set is a relatively simple task. X_2 or X_3 are instructed merely to half-contest the corner shot attempt by any of the three remaining offensive players. *Never is an attempt made to block the field goal attempt.* In some instances, we even encourage the 15-foot to 18-foot corner shot by having the low defender take no more than one or two steps in the direction of the shooter until this player demonstrates the confidence and ability to score consistently from this area. Also, we inform our low men on the triangle not to contest the pass to the corner if it is directed to a "non-shooter." Such a pass is, in reality, a non-penetrating action and is permitted according to the rules of triangular zone operation.

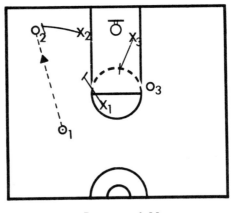

Diagram 4-11

Diagram 4-11 describes the completed shift to the corner, with X_2 out on the ball as the pass is made from O_1 to the corner. The important segment of this shift lies with X_1 and X_3 once the pass has been completed. They are both obligated to concentrate on the actions of O_3. Assuming that O_3 remains stationary, X_1 must slide low and toward the ball, while X_3 drops ball side and positions himself accordingly so as to be able to gain good inside rebound position if O_2 should decide to shoot.

On the good offensive teams, O_3 will seldom remain stationary. He would undoubtedly be in motion and preferably moving toward the ball. Such a situation would thus involve careful positioning of both X_1 and X_3 in relation to their designated areas of responsibility and that of the basketball. In Diagram 4-12 it is essential that O_3 not be permitted to cut "over the top" (as shown by the dotted lines), but forced to make his cut on the baseline. Forcing this alteration is chiefly the job of X_1 as he attempts to front O_3 on a proposed cut through the free-throw line area. Once he is forced to move low (baseline), X_3 is free to go with him since he no longer must worry about rebound position on the weak side as there is nobody occupying this area of the court. X_3 must play his man three-quarter around while he is on the move in order to nullify his total activity.

Diagram 4-12

There are several theories on corner coverage using the inverted triangle formation. However, most of these center around either bringing the Base defender out to contest the possible shot and dropping off the opposite high defender to fill the void (see Diagram 4-13), or dropping the ball-side high defender to the corner and having the remaining high defender fill the void (Diagram 4-14).

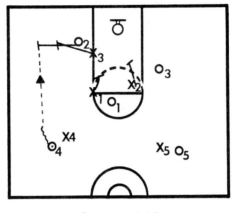

Diagram 4-13

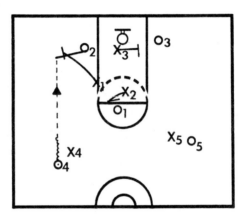

Diagram 4-14

If the Base defender is reasonably quick and alert, the standard shifting principles would be applicable. In Diagram 4-13, the shifting rules have dictated that X_3 shift with the ball near the side of the key lane. As 0_4 passes to 0_2 in the corner, X_3 (Base) need take only two or three steps toward his opponent and raise his hand to defend the shot. He does not go beyond this point for the same reasons cited regarding defender-coverage using the low-base triangle. Also, from this distance should the ball be reversed, he is able to retreat quickly to an appropriate defensive position.

Corner coverage by dropping off X_1 follows many of the shifting concepts and procedures governing the Diamond-and-One with either an immobile post player or an injured performer they wish to "hide" in the defensive set. In this particular circumstance, X_1 and X_2 become virtual chasers and are constantly on the move to protect the perimeter. As in the similar situation for the Diamond, this maneuver is not recommended for any prolonged period of time. It is intended solely for temporary use and should never be overdone since there is no assurance of permanence. The physical capacity of the players involved will be strained too far and soon the triangle will be open to exploitation.

Drilling for shifting technique

To teach the fundamental shifting procedures correctly, it is often necessary to devise several simple, yet complementary, drills for use during the practice sessions. Two such drills we have found useful over the years are modifications of other more complex drills, but have proved successful with the players. For lack of better terminology we have labeled them: "The Penetrator" and "The Pick."

The major function of "The Pick" is, of course, to work on sliding through, around, and over the various types of screens which the triangle defenders will encounter. A secondary point, which is of almost equal value in our teaching process, is the reaction of the triangle defenders who are not directly involved with the screens used by the offense. Three offensive and defensive players are involved in this half-court exercise. The actual drill begins with the offensive point bringing the ball into play with the dribble. The side to which he is forced (because of declaration pressure) becomes the side upon which the pick will be set for the man opposite the ball to use as he sees fit. Diagram 4-15 sets forth the off-ball shifts required of the triangle defenders.

"The Penetrator" is used for both the Diamond and triangle zone combinations during our daily practice periods since it is chiefly designed to teach reaction and recovery in the middle areas of these specific zones. As pictured in Diagram 4-16, the ball is passed around the perimeter of the zone and the corresponding shifts are made according to the rules. No restriction is placed on the three offensive players. The cuts to the middle will not all be of the off-ball variety, but since a

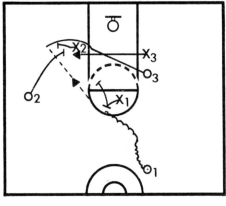

Diagram 4-15

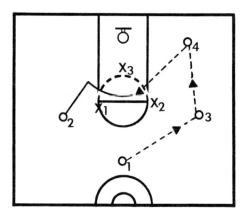

Diagram 4-16

majority of the attacking philosophies use this method, we concentrate on it heavily. In addition, we prefer the offense to pass the ball five or six times prior to attempting a field goal from a penetrating position on the floor. The offense attempts to break into the middle at every juncture and receive one of the penetrating passes for the short scoring opportunity.

After running this drill for several days, our players have fully realized the importance of keeping their hands moving on defense in order to clog the passing lanes to the inside. When the triangle defenders feel comfortable during this drill, its degree of difficulty can be altered by adding one or two more offensive players, thus forcing the defense to shift even more thoughtfully and quickly. From a coaching standpoint, it is not only important to evaluate carefully the daily drill progress, but also to be able to call the players' attention to various adaptations which the different teams may employ.

Our prime philosophy in drill sessions has been to *keep the various drills purposeful, simple, and varied* so that the players will maintain a high degree of interest in team defense.

CONTINUOUS TRIANGLE MATCH-UPS

Because of the never-ending attempts by the offense to split, gap, and overload the prescribed triangle zone, it is imperative that the defense be able to compensate for this action. All combinations must be properly matched to the offense if they are to retain any form of strength. To accomplish this, there must be a simple means to facilitate the constant match-ups necessary to cope with the offensive maneuvers.

When employing the three-man zone combinations, we have found it very helpful to label the specific positions for the players. Therefore, there is no confusion when it comes time to present an odd (one-man) or even (two-man) front to the offense. In our system, two players will have permanance—one will be designated the High defender and one the Base defender. The remaining individual assumes the role of Match-up defender and is responsibile for rotating to complete the match-up.

Of the three players, the lone High defender has the least responsibility since he must concentrate only on his specific area of coverage and the declaration. The Base unquestionably has the greatest mental burden, for he must signal out the match-up responsibility, call out the proper declaration on the ball, and cover his assigned area. The Match-up defender must, of course, make the necessary shift (which he usually can do on his own once he familiarizes himself with the various ploys of the offensive team) and either declare on the ball or merely cover his defensive zone area.

An examination of Diagram 4-17 depicts a typical split attempt with strong-side action by the offense. Faced with such a situation, the continuous matching concept allows for easy adjustment. The perma-

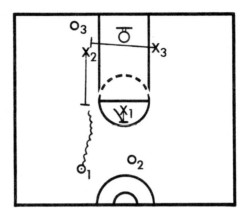

Diagram 4-17

nent Base (X_3) notes the need for correct declaration by either X_1 or X_2, depending upon which of the offensive players brings the ball into the perimeter of the zone. X_1 obviously cannot make the declaration, because he does not always know which side of the low-base set the Match-up defender is playing. The job of the Base defender in assigning the declaration is made more pronounced. Thus, X_2 initiates the declaration and in the time it takes for the Match-up defender to get to the ball, the low-base triangle has inverted itself to counter the adjustment of the offense.

During the early season practices, it is highly recommended that your team show the low-base set (within whatever other conventional defense you choose, if any) and have the Match-up defender make his adjustment with the ball in front of him. This is the easiest and most fundamental method of learning this concept. Once he and his teammates learn to work well together on this level, they will be able to handle the match-ups from the inverted set to the low areas.

CHAPTER 5

Coaching Special Combinations

Regardless of the endless variety of zone and combination match-ups employed by the defense, coaches occasionally discover that they need another dimension to complement their attack. The search for an additional defensive ploy or maneuver, for whatever purpose, can lead to a variety of unusual combination tactics. Existing in the mind of every coach is the desire to devise that sure "stopper" once the opposition has been forced into a vulnerable position. Depending on the dedication to the combination philosophy, there is a combination for every occasion.

It must be recognized that all such special combination defenses have limited scopes of effectiveness, as do any of the more familiar combinations we have previously noted. *Special tactics such as these defenses can and should be reserved for only temporary utilization.* Consequently, they fall into the category of high-risk maneuvers. The majority of these highly specialized combinations rank as gambles in that they do not possess the firm fundamental foundations found in the more conventional combinations such as the Box-and-One, Diamond-and-One and the various Triangle sets.

As with any defensive or offensive segment, one cannot "go to the well too long or too often." The over-exposure of any phase of combination defensive basketball will noticeably weaken the total counter-structure you are attempting to build. Here are several situations which could require altering the defensive aspect of the game:

1. Overpowering personnel and pattern movement of the opposition.

2. A momentary ploy to disguise, distract, or confuse the pattern flow of the opponent—throw them off-balance.

3. As a gamble to exert an unusual degree of pressure variance on the offense.

There are undoubtedly numerous other situations where a coach might consider placing his defensive trust in a special combination, or a series of combinations and standard defenses for a specific period of time. Both his desire to experiment and the means by which he attempts to command game tempo will ultimately lead to the course he will follow, since he alone knows the capabilities of his ball club.

Along this same vein lies the fact that since these defenses are usually periodic in nature, they are seldom practiced or accorded much attention during the pre-game workouts. For many teams this could be a definite drawback, so much so that they would be ill-advised to perform any such adaptation-type defense. However, for the multi-talented and fundamentally sound combination-oriented ball club, simple adjustments involving the more specialized combinations are easily made. Most of these adjustments are relatively simple. All that is required is a close adherence to the rules of combination theory.

The range of a team's overall defense is one phase of the game of basketball which is, unfortunately, overlooked during the daily practice sessions. The ability to mix your defenses serves as a good checkpoint when evaluating the progress of your defensive flexibility. It is primarily in this realm that we use many of these specialized combinations in our practice plans. If a team cannot perform the designated adjustment and appears somewhat confused about its coverage responsibilities, this usually indicates a breakdown in comprehension and some form of review and re-assessment is necessary. On the other hand, if the players demonstrate the knowledge to pass these checkpoints and make these adaptations, they will have opened a new scope of defensive tactics and their confidence both in the combination system and in themselves will soar.

THREE-MAN ZONE VARIATIONS

1. "Y Zone"

The formation set of this particular defensive adjustment reflects that of the standard low-base triangle combination. Diagram 5-1

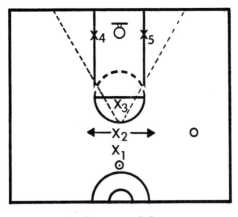

Diagram 5-1

illustrates how the perimeter coverage of this three-man zone is comparable to the other low-based triangular arrangements discussed in Chapter 4. Movement of the defense is initiated as X_1 stops the ball beyond the perimeter—eight to ten feet above the top of the key. As the declaration on the ball is made, X_2 assumes the responsibility for taking the first pass from O_1. His specific coverage area thus extends from sideline to sideline. Naturally, this is also true for X_1.

Once X_2 has approached the man with the ball, X_1 drops low and assumes the position vacated by X_2. Depending on the game situation, neither of the passes out front is pressured too heavily since they are not penetrating passes and not direct thrusts toward the goal. This emphasis of pressure can easily be altered by overplaying the exterior passing lanes and bringing up the triangle defenders into the action areas. Note that both X_1 and X_2 operate strictly beyond the pre-established perimeter and also outside the dotted line in the diagram unless the offense floods an area by sending more than three players inside the triangle. Since this combination zone does not have any assigned single-coverage duties *per se* for the exterior defenders, it cannot really be considered much of a combination in the true sense of the word.

The defensive play of the three members forming the low-base triangle is essentially the same as with any of the previously mentioned triangles. An exception does exist when the amount of pressure these defenders are forced to exert on the ball in their area is increased. The degree of pressure application must often be much greater using this

semi-combination because of the fact that true single-coverage responsibility is non-existent. As a result of this situation, *the zone members
are obligated to play the people in their area tighter than normal
(either halving or three-quartering them) whenever the ball is one pass
removed from their coverage area.*

Supporting rationale for utilizing such a specialized combination, or semi-combination defense, as this is basically two-fold: (1)
when you are facing a poor ballhandling team with a perimeter offensive pattern and desire to place additional pressure directly on the ball
out higher and force them to use more passes than they are accustomed
to get the ball into pattern alignment, thus increasing the possibility of
error; and (2) when you are in a position where you either can afford to
gamble or because of the game situation you are forced into a gambling
game and do not wish to concede any rebounding strength underneath.
We have also gone to this defensive maneuver during a close ball game
for two minutes or so just to rest our guards. With another set of guards
doing the chasing out front and harassing play, in the form of the
opposition's perimeter offensive guards, our players can come back
well-rested and instructed on what course of action to pursue next.

Diagram 5-2 shows the shifting of the Y-Zone as it prepares to
encounter an attack from out front. Here, 0_1 is quickly picked up and
guarded by X_1, who in turn, decides to pass to 0_4, breaking out from
the triangle zone. X_2 immediately slides over to pick him up and
procedes to remain with him until he either passes to a teammate or
shoots the ball himself: then resumes his position of responsibility back
into the middle.

Consequently, if 0_4 should decide to pass back to 0_1 out front,
X_1 must assume coverage in this area. The same would apply if 0_2
should break through to the opposite corner—outside the dotted line
—to create an offensive overload (see Diagram 5-3). Meanwhile, the
triangle will shift or "hedge" in accordance with combination triangle
play toward the ball at all times, with the various overplays in effect.

As mentioned at the outset of this chapter, such defensive adjustments are high-risk in nature. The Y-zone is no exception and it
does have the usual triangle weaknesses. However, its additional soft
spot stems from the very core of its strength. Both the exterior defenders, X_1 and X_2, will tire rapidly because of the expansive area they
must cover. They cannot be expected to keep this pressure up for a
prolonged length of time and once they are even slightly weakened, the

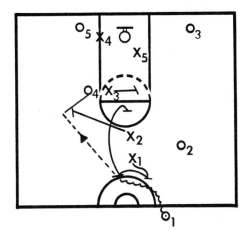

Diagram 5-2

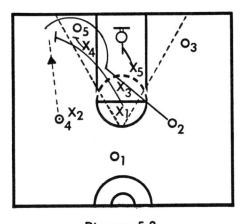

Diagram 5-3

three-man zone subsequently becomes porous because of the lack of declaration pressure out front. One must know when to call this defense off and go on to another phase of his defensive game plan. If it is done too late, it is just a matter of time until the defense is riddled from both the inside and outside.

2. "Chaser Triangle"

Once again the low-based triangle set is used as the back-up combination zone. As with the other adaptations using the triangle base, the formation of the triangle zone in this case is not allowed full match-up privileges. The primary value in running this combination is to curtail an offense which operates low, in tight to the goal, and has virtually no perimeter movement. An additional factor favoring this combination alignment is that it allows your big men to gain a breather on defense for a short period of time.

Basically, the chaser triangle has an adequate degree of fundamental stability, e.g. goal protection and mobility. Foremost among the operation principles of this adaptation is that the "chaser" (X_1) must always be between the ball and the basket (Diagram 5-4). With the constant shifting of X_2 and X_3, this positioning can be accomplished with reasonable success providing that X_1 is not only quick afoot, but is allowed to use the cross-step in approaching his man.

Diagram 5-4

Thus, the role of the "chaser" is to lend inside help to counter the offensive strength in this area. He does this at the risk of conceding the 15-foot shot on occasion near the free-throw line area, if he does not receive sufficient return help from both the low defender on the zone opposite the ball and also the single-coverage defender opposite the ball. Hopefully this "help" will avoid the problem encountered by common offensive tactics such as the split—sending two men into a single defensive area.

Perhaps the most negative aspect of this particular adjustment centers around the obvious fact that the "chaser" will tire quickly since he is forced to cover such a large area. The durability and strength of this triangular set could greatly be enhanced by the built-in match-up concept. This would unquestionably decrease its vulnerability when withstanding any carefully planned assault by the offense.

When obligated by circumstances to resort to such a defense, it is strongly recommended that the coach have an alternative plan up his sleeve to come back with, once the chaser adaptation shows any sign of weakening. Since the amount of time one can expect to get out of this type of tactic is relatively short, many coaches feel that such defenses are not worth the practice time spent in preparation. If this attitude prevails, no adaptations should ever be tried during a game since this would be in direct opposition to the individual defensive philosophy. However, these defenses are occasionally necessary and if a team can get one or two minutes of game play from them at a strategic point, they are indeed a valuable asset to possess.

3. "Rotating Invert Match-up"

During the past four seasons we have found this aspect of the three-man zone combination to be one of the most effective because of the extensive coverage it affords the interior zone area. By means of rotating the defenders within the confines of the triangle, not only is the mid-section continually covered, there is also constant movement to add to the offensive problem of penetration. When single-coverage is directed against the opposition's post man, it virtually assures that the key area will be cluttered and therefore is nullified as a primary attacking area. Thus, the offense will be forced to concentrate its thrust elsewhere. Because of its unique shifting process, this form of the triangle zone is the most difficult for the opposing teams to pick up. Therefore, we have been able to get a great deal of mileage out of it since we can stay with it longer than most of the other adaptations we have hitherto discussed. Another outstanding characteristic of this combination is that it can also be easily disguised within the popular match-up zone defenses.

This floating, or rotating triangle is automatically matched to the offensive set in accordance with the rules set forth in Chapter 4. Therefore, the defense can set with either the low-base or the inversion to begin the rotation. It makes little difference as to which, since the initial rotation of the three-man zone will dictate all corresponding shifts. Adhering strictly to triangle defensive theory, an attempt is made to retain the shape of the triangle at all times with the interior defenders . . . the top men (man) always on the ball when it is being handled by a player who is not individually covered. *The rotation is contingent upon the defender taking the ball in his area until it is stopped or passed.* The remaining two men in the triangle must float/hedge toward the ball action while keeping tabs on the offensive personnel in their specific coverage areas.

When the ball is *driven* to another area (Diagram 5-5), the original defender (X_2) must stay with the dribbler. Once the ball is stopped, X_2 has become one of the low defenders. X_3 takes X_2's former position in the triangle, and X_1 shifts in order to give weak side help and watch for cutters low.

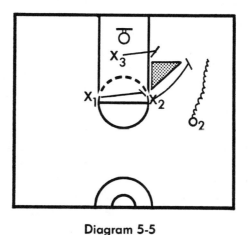

Diagram 5-5

As the ball is *passed* to another area, it becomes the responsibility of the nearest defender. In Diagram 5-6, that would be X_3. The only concerns of the triangle men are sliding toward the ball and retention of the triangle shape. Note that in this diagram, X_3 forces his man to the inside where he can get help from both X_2 and X_1.

Diagrams 5-7 and 5-8 illustrate how the triangle players interchange to cover passes around the perimeter of the triangle following the established rotation rules. Because of this lateral movement by the defense, the inverted alignment is extremely difficult to penetrate once rotation begins.

The triangle provides excellent interior rebounding position.

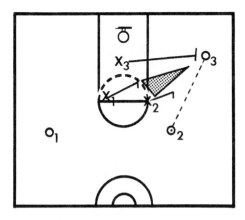

Diagram 5-6

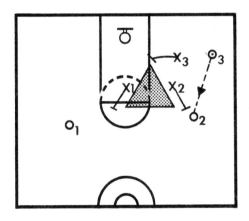

Diagram 5-7

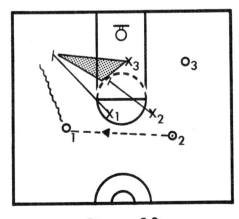

Diagram 5-8

Additional rebound help can also be afforded by the single-coverage players since they are expected to contact (screen out) their men as far outside as possible and hold them out of the rebounding area. We have found it best to have our three big men play the positions of the triangle, but size makes little difference in setting up the initial triangle because all three defenders must rotate according to ball flow. The only essential qualifications we insist on for our zone players are that they be able to shift quickly without taking their eyes off both the ball and the man in their area, and know how to screen out and rebound.

TWO-MAN ZONE COMBINATIONS

The two-man zone modifications differ only slightly from the examples cited for the three-man zone combinations. Here too, the combination principles remain intact, but they must be even more carefully adhered to than ever. To be a truly effective defensive counterforce, *the two-man zone can never afford to be static (set), but rather a continuum of match-ups for the opponent to cope with*. The screening and gapping tactics used by a majority of the modern offenses make this continuous adjustment absolutely necessary.

Many coaches have casually disgarded the two-man zone combination as "just another combination adjustment" without full consideration of what this specific combination can and cannot do. There are numerous occasions when the two-man zone serves a useful purpose. For example, because of the three "denial" defenders operating on the perimeter, a more concentrated degree of pressure can be exerted on the entire offense, not merely on one or two individuals. It is only to be expected that the three single-coverage players can cause more havoc than two, as in the triangle zone variations, thus causing more pattern disruption. Also, by employing a defense such as this, the ability to execute the double-team (trap) situation—either by the three exterior man-to-man defenders, or by involving one of the zone members—is greatly enhanced. (We will note this in more detail below.) In addition to the above advantages, simple switching on the perimeter can be accomplished automatically without fear of serious repercussion.

Perhaps the most dynamic utilization factor of this dimension of combination basketball is achieved when it is applied against a team with a weak inside attack. Two interior zone defenders will usually be more than sufficient to counter any offensive maneuver such a team can mount. This becomes an even more pronounced possible curtailment when the zone defenders are assured that they will always receive weak-side "help" from the "denial" man farthest from the ball. Furthermore, this zone combination can also guarantee some measure of rebounding stability as a result of the interior zone match-ups coupled with the sag effect of the off-ball "denial" defenders.

Basic operating rules governing the two-man zone center around the following:

1. Show a match-up zone interior—either vertically or horizontally—and attempt to retain a match-up throughout the offensive thrust (Diagram 5-9).

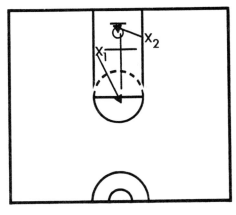

Diagram 5-9

2. The zone defenders should seldom extend themselves more than one step beyond the confines of the key lane to defend the man in their assigned area.

3. Both zone players must constantly "hedge" toward the ball with direct overplay action on the ball side.

4. The low defenders are also responsibile for cutters in their respective areas and for verbally informing their teammates concerning the approaching screens and situations.

5. *Regarding switching:* This is permitted only when the defender is not able to slide through, or fight over, a pick. Beyond the designated perimeter, there is never any switching allowed away from the ball. The jump switch is used on the ball only when necessary, although we attempt to discourage even this tendency as much as physically possible.

6. Overplay only the possible penetrating passing lanes.

Transforming this combination from an area defense into a ball defense is much more easily accomplished than with any of the other combination defenses. Since there are three "denial" defenders, they may choose to trap at any given time and place with the built-in assurance that if their defensive assignment should get loose for a return pass out of the trap, the interior zone members will pick them up until they are able to recover.

Trapping from the 3:2 combination is indeed a valuable tool, although it must be enacted with a certain amount of caution. When you are behind, or tied, in a close contest and desire to force the opposition into a turnover or jump-ball situation, the double-team can be put into motion. As stated earlier, the traps can be made by either two of the single-coverage players or by one of the zone members and a "denial" defender.

Diagram 5-10 illustrates the trapping sequence versus the often-used blind-side screen-and-cut; most common in the various shuffle offenses. In this particular pattern, O_3 attempts to free himself by rubbing his man off on the pick set by O_1. According to the rules, X_1 should pick up all the penetrating cutters if they should lose their man. If this were the case, X_1 would be obligated to remain with O_3 until the "denial" man recovered and both men could then effect the trap on the ball. Once such a trap is activated, it becomes the responsibility of all the defenders, not merely those in the zone, to plug all the passing lanes within visibility of the man with the ball. (Note the positioning of X_5 as the trap is made.) Both X_5 and X_4 are the true keys to the success or failure of the trap because they must be able to situate themselves so that they can pick off the pass attempts from O_3 to his teammates.

Trapping without involving the zone players is by far the simplest means of placing additional pressure on the offensive workhorses. This can be done in typical man-to-man fashion with the two

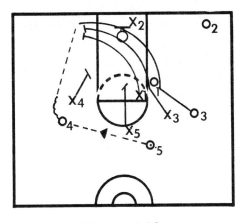

Diagram 5-10

nearest players to the ball performing the trap and the remaining defenders responsible for plugging the passing lanes and taking a chance at intercepting one of the passes thrown under pressure. The only requirement for perimeter trapping centers on the player who is leaving his assigned man to make the trap. He is only to attempt a trap when the player handling the ball cannot see him—has his back to the trapper.

THE CENTER, ONE-MAN, OR PRO-ZONE

Although the rules of professional basketball strictly prohibit the use of the zone defense in any way, shape, or form, the carefully trained eye can observe its practice upon occasion. Justification for such a ruling is that it would undoubtedly take away some of the truly great individual styles and individual match-ups which the paying customer desires to see. ''The zones, match-ups, or combination zones, would serve to reduce the pace of the game and also lessen its appeal.''

Suffice it to say, these types of zones, semi-zones, and endless combinations of the one-man variety do exist at the professional level and are gradually filtering down to the colleges and high schools today. With the size of today's post man, those coaches fortunate enough to have the good big man want to do everything in their power to keep him near the basket, both offensively and defensively. If this can be accomplished, the middle (key area) can be virtually controlled by a single player. There is no question as to the advantageous position this creates for the defense. Consequently, the other four defenders are granted more freedom and thus the defense becomes much more versatile in its adjustments and tactics. There will be more switching and trapping on the perimeter since there will no longer be the fear of the pick-and-roll situation. (This is evidenced, also, more and more in the pro game.) An additional plus for the center zone is that it can readily be disguised as a straight man-to-man or zone match-up and thus accommodates itself nicely to lend the appearance of the combination zones.

The successful operation of this form of defensive basketball is entirely dependent upon two things: the reaction ability of the post man and the amount of "help-side" assistance he receives from the four man-to-man players. Basically, the job of the post is rather simple in that he is responsible for:

1. The man in his area with emphasis on "ball-you-man" positioning.
2. All primary cutters through the key, especially those cutters only one pass removed from the ball.
3. Keeping his arms up to deflect penetrating passes inside.
4. Calling out all upcoming picks on his teammates out front.

Once the opposition figures out what the defense is and plans a counter move, it is time to consider another defense. The most frequent method of attacking the center zone is to overload the sides, or angles, and thereby attempt to create a one-on-one situation inside. However, if there is adequate "help" from the man ("denial") farthest from the ball, this action can be countered and quickly discouraged.

The most advantageous use of this combination formation lies with its employment against a team with a weak inside game. In Diagram 5-11, the pick-and-roll situation created by the switch of X_5 and X_4 cannot effectively take place because of the positioning of the center-zone defender. Should O_4 try to roll to the goal and look for the return pass, he would automatically find himself covered. X_1 is able to leave his primary responsibility since he is assured of weak-side

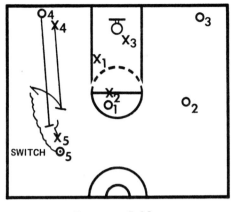

Diagram 5-11

"help" from X_2 and X_3. With the elimination of the pick-and-roll, many an offense can become quite static and limited in its scope of attack.

ATTACKING THE COMBINATIONS

With the increasing popularity of the combination-style defenses, the task of preparing a team to recognize, react, and counter the various forms of the combinations is essential to total team planning. Our purpose here, obviously, is not to offer detailed offensive theory in coping with these unique defenses, but rather to alert the defense-oriented coach to several of the more frequently tried and tested means of combating them. *Every team must possess an alternative, quick-hitting offensive pattern designed to put points on the board when they find their familiar continuity disrupted.*

Regardless of the offensive approach set forth to confront a particular combination, it should initially be placed into operation from a pre-matched formation. Since the defense will undoubtedly attempt to match the offensive set, it thus becomes imperative that the offense capitalize on this fact. Therefore, *the alternative offensive plan (movement) must be made from the original formation.* Ideally, one or two passes should be enough to allow the offense to get into their attacking position.

There are four commonly applied tactics acknowledged as sound alternatives in dealing with combination defenses:

1. Freeing Key Single-Coverage Players
   —screens set for their use
   —using them as decoys and screeners
   —creating mis-matches by forcing switches

2. Forcing False Declarations by the Defense
   —described in Chapters 2-4

3. Gaining Deeper/more Advantageous Penetration
   —frontal maneuvers as mentioned earlier in this chapter
     and in Chapter 4
   —driving the ball into the side of the overload

4. Directing the Attack toward Vulnerable Areas in the Semi-zone
   —gapping and splitting the front
   —overloading
   —freeing cutters to specific areas

Perhaps the single most perplexing problem facing the defense with regard to the above is that dealing with the means of freeing players for a good percentage shot at the goal. This is by far the least sophisticated means of attack, yet continues to redirect pressure back to the defense.

Against both the three and four-man combination zones, the "pop-out" move is considered one of the best means of freeing non-single-covered players for an open shot within a prescribed perimeter. Diagram 5-12 shows that a move such as this forces the single-coverage defender to switch if he is not able to fight over or through the pick. Two things become apparent when this maneuver is analyzed: (1) as the switch occurs, the "denial" player must pick up the taller of the two individuals and a mismatch has been created; (2) much to the advantage of the offense, the interior defender is now confronted with the task of having to handle one of the offense's more powerful performers. As a coach facing this situation, there are three realistic courses of action open—one of which includes permitting the situation above to transpire and hope for the best. That, of course, would be utter folly! The remaining choices are to concede O_3 the uncontested shot, thus leaving the single-coverage on O_5 intact, or to insist that X_3 leave the confines of his area and fight through the screen and get to his

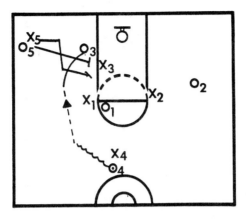

Diagram 5-12

main responsibility which would seriously jeopardize the interior of the semi-zone.

Speaking from a strictly defensive standpoint, the only percentage choice in Diagram 5-12 would be to concede the shot until such time that another decision (from the bench) occurs. O_3 is permitted the shot, or at least the opportunity to get the shot off, until he hits several shots in a row. The decision to permit the shot here is in keeping with the roots of our basic philosophy of forcing the non-stars to carry the offensive burden.

Diagram 5-13 exhibits one of the more frequently applied tactics used to counter and attack the Box-and-One. In this particular instance, the pattern run by the player who receives "denial" coverage is a type of weave, or figure-eight. He will run this pattern according to the strengths of his shooting areas. For example, a forward would run the low pattern and a guard would operate a higher pattern. It is quite possible for a player who favors one side of the court to run this type of move solely in this area also. He can be momentarily freed if one of the offensive players gives him a good pick. A majority of these picks are actually moving screens, but since this player is usually moving away from the ball to set up his pick, they are seldom seen or called by the officials. With this tactic in mind, the four offensive players are virtually given a green light to "head-hunt" the single-coverage defender when he is in their area.

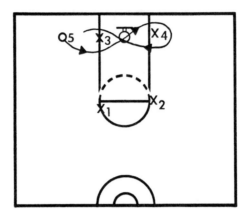

Diagram 5-13

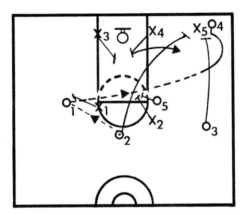

Diagram 5-14

A third screening concept involves using the original offensive pattern and merely switching personnel to set up a given (controlled) situation; *i.e.*, using the offensive star as a decoy. In this case (Diagram 5-14), O_4 is a sharpshooting guard who takes his man to the low corner away from the ball. As the ball is moved opposite him, the Box shifts accordingly as shown. To make the zone more honest, O_1 will look for the drive to the goal, forcing both X_3 and X_4 to shift. Meanwhile, X_5 must be aware of the position of the ball in relation to his man and glances to the inside for a brief moment. As this is done, both

O_2 and O_3 set up a double pick for O_4, who cuts over the top to his favorite shooting area. O_5 further protects the area with a quick pick on X_5 inside the three-second lane. If X_4 should take it upon his shoulders to come out high and attempt to stop O_4, both O_2 and O_3 would have a clear and almost uncontested lane to the basket for a return pass from O_4. The same applies if X_2 should try and come out high—O_5 is free on the inside. This is, indeed, a most difficult maneuver to defend and can only be truly curtailed by having X_5 fight through the picks and anticipate such screening action.

These methods of attack will be as diverse as the defenses they are designed to counter and can be challenged only by a flexible combination that can match up to the original set and thereby move as the offense moves. As a defensive coach, you must anticipate the offensive alternative and be prepared to cope with it. The careful teaching of the shifting techniques and emphasis on weak-side "help" can go a long way in handling the offensive thrust. The fundamentally sound combination system can do more than prevail in these situations, it can dominate when employed with necessary discretion.

CHAPTER 6

Disguising the Combinations in a Multiple Defensive System

The decision to play combination defensive basketball is dictated, as mentioned in earlier chapters, by numerous factors. However, once it has been established that this type strategy is best suited to a given situation, the option exists to extend the scope of the team's strongest combination one step further. Regardless of the specific set combination chosen for deployment, it will be quickly picked up by the astute coaches of the opposition and, in most cases, by their players. In order to get more mileage from any particular combination which you feel to be one of your team's greatest assets, it should be carefully camouflaged within the confines of a more recognizable zone defense. Whether or not the offense is able to counter this defensive maneuver effectively is a matter of speculation, but it will continually keep them off-guard.

Most team quarterbacks, or playmakers, can quickly spot the conventional 1:2:2, 1:3:1, and the 2:1:2 zones, especially if the zone members are tightly knit with their arms moving in the passing lanes. Usually upon detection, either the coach or the playmaker will instinctively react to the offensive zone options designed to split the seams of this particular zone defense. *Such is precisely the situation/impression that you want your defense to create!* After he is shown the standard zone set two or three times down the floor, the opponent is somewhat relaxed and confident with his zone attack methodology and the time is now appropriate for the zone to vary its shifting techniques only slightly to throw off the opposition. One or two "minor" shifting adjustments will readily set in motion many of the pre-designed combination defenses selected for use as the team's best counterforce.

It has only been during the past few seasons that we have actively sought to disguise the combination defenses in this fashion. However, we are reasonably well satisfied with the results. This is especially so with the additional length of service we have been able to get from our stronger combination match-ups. Formerly, it seemed sufficient to employ any of the combinations and go with it until it was successfully attacked. There was never any attempt to disguise this defense since it was such a devastating force by itself.

Aside from the previously mentioned time-factor justification, there are four other arguments for using a camouflage system. The false/shell defenses enable the combinations to become:

1. *More effective by their appearance.* Their deceptive appearance can be varied and shifted in a variety of ways and also from numerous positions within the defense.

2. *Easily operative.* This technique can be simply implemented into any defensive system. Teaching the fundamentals of this method centers around one major rule; fill the void and cover the area!

3. *Highly functional and also durable.* When properly employed, such a system can withstand much offensive pressure as well as add a degree of security to the overall defense.

4. *Self-motivating.* From a coaching standpoint, this system is both interesting and intriguing and perpetuates player interest.

As far as many fine coaches are concerned, the idea of camouflaging the defense is the direct counterpart to the "initial moves" used to propel the primary offense. Just as the good offensive teams have several alternative "initial moves" at their disposal to set up the offense, the good defensive teams must likewise possess several such "moves" prior to settling into their desired defensive pattern.

At this time, it is important to consider two frequently mentioned statements:

Coaching philosophy is a matter of personal selection!

The culmination of the master plan for any athletic contest is
defensive preparation!

The two statements are totally inter-related since the philosophy of any
defensive plan will always be a variable becuase of the infinite variety
of situations teams are required to meet. If any parallel to coaching
basketball exists, it is the championship chess match between two
master players. The commitment to planning and counter-planning can
never be too great or exacting. Perhaps the following account will
enable the reader to judge the "chess-game" philosophy of team defense:

> The scouting report on one of the teams in our
> league indicated that they operate from a 1:3:1 offensive set
> and have an excellent All-League player at the wing who is
> a fine perimeter shooter, currently averaging 20 points per
> game. The remaining starters and early substitutes are all
> fair outside shooters, but only tokenly attack the offensive
> boards. Their 1:3:1 offense is a total continuity pattern.
>
> Our primary philosophy was obviously to hold their
> star intact, prevent interior offensive penetration after the
> initial shot, and force them to make some adjustments in
> their pattern execution, while allowing their four other
> players their normal shot selection. Therefore, the game
> philosophy and defensive preparation were as follows:

1. We began the game using a straight 1:3:1 zone with
   attention focused on their star wherever he was with the
   ball. Our players had their hands high as they dropped
   into the goal defense to enable the opposition's point-
   man to call for the zone offense set (Diagram 6-1). Their
   initial step in countering this zone set was to split the top
   of our zone, thus forcing us to match up with a corresponding two-man front (Diagram 6-2).

2. Our two-man front zone (with three deep defenders)
   permitted them to attack according to plan for the first
   couple of field goals by their star—O_4.

3. Once their star hit his second field goal, which happened
   to be the number we had decided upon before the game,
   "denial" coverage would be placed on him once he
   crossed the 21-foot perimeter, or the ball was brought
   across mid-court, whichever occurred first.

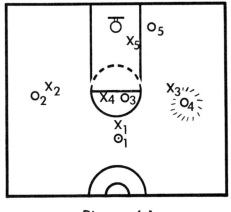

Diagram 6-1

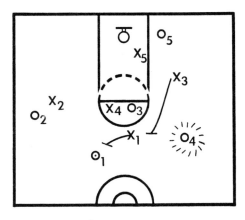

Diagram 6-2

4. After several attempts at the basket, the opposition's star performer established his shooting areas—just above the free-throw line extended. As we declared on the point, single-coverage had taken place by the nearest high defender on the zone (X_3). He then continued about his assigned "denial" task and the middle zone defender simply assumed his vacated position on the wing. Upon completion of this shift, we were now showing the original defensive front that matched up with their power offense, while taking their outstanding offensive player out of the pattern. The Diamond also provided us with

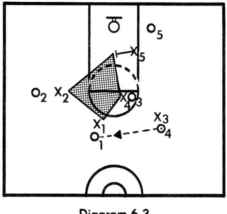

Diagram 6-3

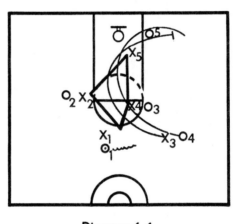

Diagram 6-4

sufficient rebounding dominance (Diagrams 6-3 and 6-4).

Because of the camouflaging and the use of a given time factor (two field goals by the opposition's star) we were able to get more than two and one-half quarters of play from our use of the Diamond-and-One combination.

By using this system of passive and active defensive techniques, we successfully forced the offense to carry out two distinct adjustments: the first versus the semi-active match-up and the second against the more aggressive combination. There is no offensive team that wants to cope with this, or be forced into the many adjustments required for survival. There is also the possibility that the offense is not fully prepared to react effectively this far in advance. More importantly, the offense is ultimately obligated to counter its attack directly into the strength of the defense.

SHIFTING PHILOSOPHIES

There are two accepted methods of enacting the shift(s) from the passive standard zone and man-to-man sets to the various active combinations. Easiest to initiate is the direct shift from the zone to the combination zone on a pre-assigned signal: first pass in the offensive pattern; first cut, or pass by the star player(s) in the continuity pattern; or by a directive from the bench. As the key is activated, the "denial" player(s) can assume responsibilities in accordance with the demands of the defense. The key (usually coded and sent in from the bench) initiates the shifts for single-coverage while the remaining members are to fill the appropriate voids in the semi-zone defense. This unquestionably is the simplest and most widely taught shifting technique in use throughout the country today.

When the primary intent of the combination is to disrupt pattern play, this concept of "pick-up-and-fill" is one of the most effective countering methods since it does allow for a variance in both the single-coverage assignment(s) and also the type(s) of combinations the coaching staff prefers to employ. With respect to the defensive game plan, this multiple system enables the team to alter the defense as often as needed, or to continue with the same combination, for as long as its desired effectiveness remains intact.

Because of the simplicity of the shifting movements, this system is a most practical approach for the majority of high school and junior college teams. With only a few practice sessions, this technique can be easily implemented if the shifting maneuvers are designed to set up single-coverage on only one player—e.g., Box or Diamond zone.

In the examples cited below, the designated offensive player (circled in the diagram) moves opposite the position set as noted in the scouting report and constitutes a like defensive lateral shift so that the

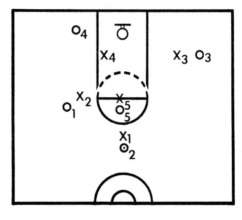

Diagram 6-5

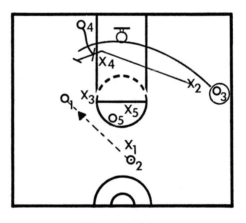

Diagram 6-6

assigned "denial" man (X₂) will be in position to assume his single-coverage duties (see Diagrams 6-5 and 6-6). Player #3 is the opposition's chief threat that must be halted once the key is activated—his initial cut to the opposite side. Single-coverage could not take place until the "denial" man (X₂) matched up to the same side of the court as his assignment and thus if 0₃ had cut to the basket and on to the ball side for the overload on their first possession, only the zone shifts associated with the 1:3:1 would have taken place. As the single-coverage is put into play, the remaining members drop into either the Box or Diamond, depending on what the defensive needs are at that time. Because of the high post used by the offense and the degree with which that particular floor position area is utilized by the offense, the decision to go with the Box or Diamond must be carefully weighed.

As mentioned above, the same simplified shifts can be made from any of the conventional zone formations. Also, two or three men can be drawn out of the zone set in a like manner to add further confusion for the offense to contain. Referring once again to Diagram 6-6, assume that player O_2, the team playmaker, also warrants single-coverage. Once the key has been activated, the "denial" defenders gain position on their men while the others maintain a match-up triangle, with X_4 in charge of the triangle defenders since the play unfolds directly in front of him (Diagram 6-7).

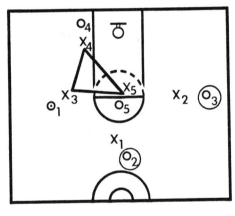

Diagram 6-7

Possessing the ability to alter defenses quickly from the passive standard zones to the more pressurized one-, two-, three-, and four-man combinations lends a tremendous amount of defensive flexibility to any team. Today's game demands this because of the sophistication and emphasis placed on offensive pattern play. Many coaches believe that a quick-shifting defense is much more effective than one which slides—going through another phase such as the match-up before arriving at the combination stage—especially if the combination is your prime defensive tactic.

A more effective, yet somewhat more complex, manner in which to execute the shifts from the straight zone(s) to the combination(s) is to fully exercise the zone match-up possibilities. This involves going one step beyond the conventional zone set and giving the appearance of constructing a match-up zone defense prior to shifting into the desired combination. There are many coaches who are thoroughly dedicated to the match-up philosophy and who will prefer to go completely through the complete match-up phase since they are firmly convinced the situation demands this action. When the match-up has run its course of effectiveness, they will finalize their defensive adjustments into a specific combination. In the following sequence of Diagrams, 6-8 through 6-11, note the manner in which the *specific needs of the defense* are met: *single-coverage* on O_3—the leading scorer; countering the *angle-shooting pattern of the opposition;* keeping X_3 *inside for defensive rebounding* purposes, and *shutting off their offensive continuity.*

Because of the complex nature of using the complete match-up concept as a segmented step to enacting the combination defenses, the method of altering the defensive front of the standard zone to match the opponents, will usually serve to create a sufficient diversion before actually shifting into the full combination. This concept has proved most successful primarily because of its relative simplicity and minimum of player rotation. As a general rule, our teams always begin with a two-man defensive front and designate one (or the only one) of the "denial" men as the match-up defender. It is his responsibility to slide or drop off, to create the actual one-man front. Thus, the majority of our standard defensive tactics center around only two of the conventional zones which makes it easy for our players to become proficient with the shifting movements associated with each. Diagram 6-12 illustrates the simple frontal shift used to match-up with the offensive set. If the offense comes down the court and immediately splits our front with a single player, our primary "denial" player (X_1) will drop off to the ball side. As this occurs, the deep defenders in the 2:1:2 come up to form a 1:3:1. Had the offense come down and not split the front, our defense would have been free to go into the pre-arranged combination at any given time.

Regardless of the shifting process that one feels most comfortable with, there are four essential points that must receive considerable

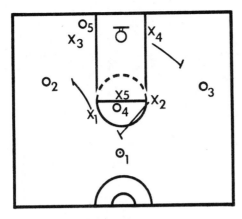

Diagram 6-8

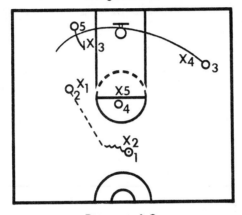

Diagram 6-9

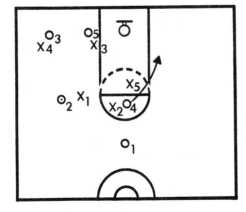

Diagram 6-10

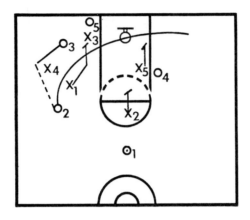

Diagram 6-11

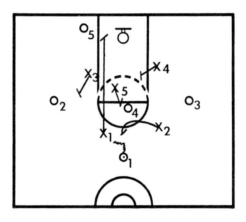

Diagram 6-12

attention before you attempt to put such a system into practice on any scale. This list includes:

1. *Simplicity*—The rules and shifting procedures must be easily understood by all team members. Keep them few in number and as "catchy" phrase-wise as possible so they are seldom forgotten in the "heat of battle." For example, "pick up-and-fill."

2. *Possibility*—Avoid commitment to unrealistic defensive shifting pattern sequences. You can do only what your

talent allows. The match-ups and the combinations must be both feasible and practical.

3. *Validity*—Are the shifts really necessary, or could you get by without using them? Don't overwork the defensive team by burdening them with unnecessary shifting. This basic premise goes hand-in-hand with the idea of overall simplicity as noted above.

4. *Variety*—Keep the total defensive system flexible by altering the active combinations you use. Vary the manner in which your team gets into the combinations: don't always initiate the shifts and "denial" coverage on the same keys! It is also a good idea to vary the single-coverage assignments to keep the offense off-guard.

A note of caution with respect to full committment to this system of adjustment centers around point number three—VALIDITY. *Shift only when it is beneficial for your total defensive game plan* and not because you believe it is the thing to do to complement your overall defensive strategy.

ZONE MATCH-UP SHIFTS INTO
THE FOUR-MAN COMBINATIONS

When it has been established that this defensive tactic is the focal point of your attack, the coaching staff must then formulate a decision on how important the assigned "denial" coverage is to the total defensive combination picture. Must this coverage be done by a specific player, or can this assignment be divided among any of two or three individuals? In a sampling of cases cited by coaches who frequently employ the four-man combination zones, they were of the opinion that *it is the semi-zone that is more of a devastating force to the opposition than the actual individual player coverage.* Assuming this to be true, the shifting phase (from the match-up to the combination) will be much easier and smoother to enact. Thus, the final shift into the Box or Diamond can usually be accomplished by using either a "fill" movement or an adaptation of the "reverse-rotation" principle.

We have previously discussed the "fill" concept as being a quick (stunt-type) shift, wherein the nearest of the selected defenders fills the void left by the player who opts out of the zone and takes up single-coverage. Almost as simple to perform is an alternate method used by teams who choose to match up their initial zone by rotating personnel. A majority of the match-up defenses are operated by either a clockwise or counter-clockwise rotation, so that each player-area of the floor is occupied by a defender. The reversal of this rotation process, as the single-coverage is taking place, will also serve to fill the gaps existing in the semi-zone.

In each of the following diagrams, a counter-clockwise rotation will be used to shift into the combination. The chief basis for choosing this type of rotation from the full match-up is fundamentally entrenched in our system since it enables us to restore the defensive symmetry we sacrificed as a result of the match-up. In our match-up system, even though seldom used, we have always initiated the actual match-up by a clockwise rotation. This, of course, is merely an example of personal preference.

Diagram 6-13 shows the clockwise rotation from the 2:1:2 zone into the match-up zone, while the following diagram (6-14) illustrates the completed shift into the Box-and-One combination using the "reverse-rotation" concept of restoring defensive balance. Assuming that O_1 is the team quarterback, and the better of the perimeter shooters, he can best be curtailed by single-coverage, when the scouting report suggests that the team offense is predicated around the low-angle shooting areas. Seemingly, it is less confusing for all players if the man nearest the assigned individual offensive star takes him on his first possession following the shift. With but one exception this is always true! The exception is when the nearest defender is our top defensive rebounder whom we cannot afford to spare for a single-coverage assignment. In this case, we will continue the match-up phase of our zone until the specific player regains ball possession outside this particular area. The results of the shift to the combination accomplish exactly what they were designed for: keeping X_3 and X_4 low for the purposes of interior rebounding security, while sealing off the lower shooting angles.

Had the situation been that of an angle-shooting team with a rather weak inside game as the target, the combination shift from the match-up would, in all likelihood, have been of the Diamond variety. Diagram 6-15 suggests that once again the same rules apply regarding the simplicity of the rotation shift to complete the Diamond. Note that

137

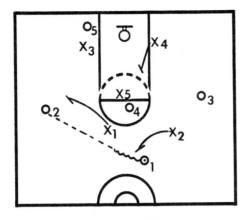

Diagram 6-13

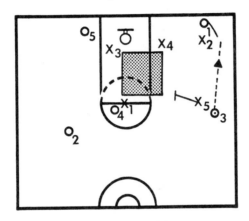

Diagram 6-14

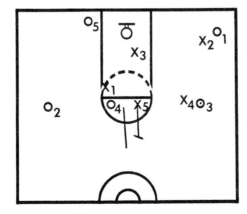

Diagram 6-15

as O_1 passes and cuts to the corner, the offense must also shift in order to provide themselves with a safety valve (to prevent the defense from gaining a quick advantage on a loose ball or intercepted pass—O_2 or O_4), which will be covered by either X_1 or X_5, according to the shifting rules governing the particular "reverse-rotation" principle employed—clockwise or counter-clockwise.

The shift from the two-man match-up front zone into the Box-and-One is perhaps the most simple of all to execute. Diagram 6-16 demonstrates the initial 1:3:1 zone having been forced into a two-man front zone by the use of a clockwise shift. "Denial" coverage is to be

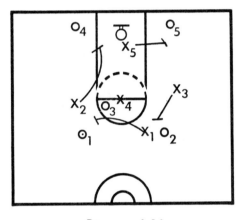

Diagram 6-16

placed on O_3, operating from the high post. Since this player is a physical-type performer with better than average height, we have schooled X_1, X_2 and X_4 (our better big men) in single-coverage play and, therefore, if O_3 should line up in a different floor position from that indicated in our scouting report after the match-up, we will be fully prepared to combat him with either of these three players. Once a sequence such as hitting the high post has occurred, the Box can be put into active motion with X_4 assuming the coverage on O_3. As is the case in this instance, there is no need for any further shifting, since floor position has been completed by the match-up. Fortunately, this circumstance happens occasionally, especially if the scouting report and pre-game planning are accurate.

Shifting from the one-man front zone to the two-man frontal match-up can also be accomplished automatically as seen in Diagram

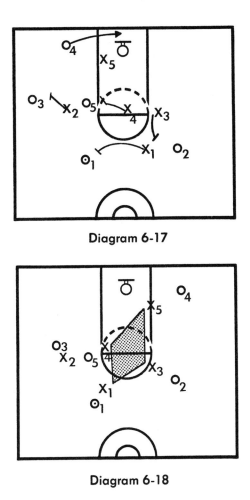

Diagram 6-17

Diagram 6-18

6-17. O_3 is again the player attracting single-coverage with the remaining members of the defense dropping into the Diamond. Diagram 6-18 clearly shows that here again there is no need for any further shifts once X_2 assumes his role as a man-to-man defender.

SHIFTING INTO THE THREE-MAN COMBINATIONS FROM THE MATCH-UP

When employing a shift of this magnitude, it must always be a smooth continuous transition. Also, it must always slide into an automatic match-up triangle zone. There are, of course, the two other triangle sets which the defense could choose, but the matching triangle is by far the most advantageous because of its active nature of total aggressiveness and also because it is the most difficult for the opposition to diagnose (see Chapter 4). Whenever the situation warrants this defensive adjustment, it can be sprung from either a man-to-man or one of the more conventional zone alignments.

Since the deployment of any pressurized combination system is designed as a temporary tactic, most coaches want to be assured that their single-coverage assignments are carefully planned. This is even more important as the number of "denial" defenders is increased. In any resulting triangle system, "denial" selectivity becomes exceedingly important because of the necessity of retaining at least two agressive rebounders within the confines of the three-man arrangement. *No shifts are to be made unless this interior rebounding concentration has been fully assured.* Every player, whether starter or substitute, must thoroughly understand this most basic of premises!

For the sake of consistency, the shifting maneuvers into the three-man zone combinations will be those beginning from the one and two-man fronts of the 1:3:1 and 2:1:2 zones. Essentially, the shifting rules for these adjustments follow virtually the same principles set forth in the previous section of the chapter dealing with the four-man zones.

As can be observed in Diagram 6-19, the defense (2:1:2) was initiated to combat the offense's two-man frontal attack. According to the scouting report, the offensive tendency was to split the defensive front of the zone. It was, therefore, only a matter of time until the defense would be forced to shift into a match-up front—by a clockwise rotation. Both O_1 and O_4 are serious enough offensive performers to demand single-coverage. After the match-up has taken place, "denial" coverage commences when either of the two players completes a pass within the continuity pattern. This defense remains intact until the coach decides to discard it for another. Both X_1 and X_2 have been prepared for the possibility that they might be called upon to take O_1, while X_5 knows he will be assigned O_4 once the key activates the shift. In completing the match-up triangle, Diagram 6-20 indicates that it becomes the low triangle defender (X_3) who must assign specific coverage responsibilities. He can only assume this role when it has been established (by the pre-game plan) that he shall be the permanent

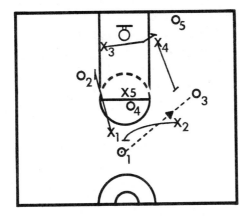

Diagram 6-19

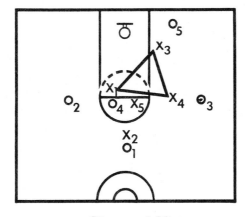

Diagram 6-20

low member of the triangle. He quickly selects one of the other semi-zone members as the match-up man and directs the flow of the particular triangle zone: a position match-up, or a rotating type.

Diagram 6-21 shows the rotation from the 1:3:1 zone into the two-man frontal match-up and the overload tactic off the reversal by the offense when they are unable to penetrate the ball. In this instance, O_1 and O_4 are the two players who merit "denial" attention and are to be attacked once either of them has handled the ball in the pattern. Should O_4 decide not to reverse the ball and in turn drive to the basket,

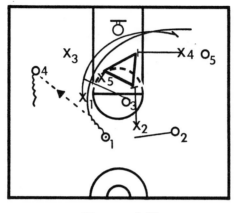

Diagram 6-21

he would have to beat both X_3 and X_4 (the low man on the triangle who would shift automatically toward the ball).

The idea of pulling two men out of any zone or man defense creates an automatic triangle situation. How this weapon is utilized is the key! There must be a real purpose/function for the members of the triangle and, above all, they must be constantly moving to gain position on the men in their area.

OTHER POPULAR SHIFTS INTO THE COMBINATIONS

Perhaps the most frequently used zone in practice today is the "bottle" or 1:2:2 zone set. This formation is one of the easiest of the passive zones from which to enact the match-up and also the combination, be it a one-, two-man front, or a triangle. In our defensive attack, we use this zone whenever we want to "hit quick" and are less concerned about camouflaging the defense. Our most frequent use of the 1:2:2 shift to the combination centers around the Box and Diamond zones because the "fill" principle is so simple to enact. Granted the means of disguise and match-up possibilities are endless when using this zone, as it is with the 1:3:1 and the 2:1:2, however, because of our preference for those zone sets, we only use the 1:2:2 for the above-mentioned reason. It does serve to give the opposition yet another view of our total defensive motion.

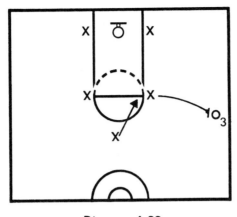

Diagram 6-22

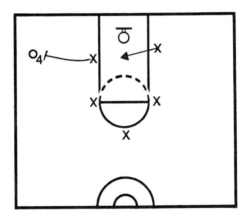

Diagram 6-23

When shifting the 1:2:2 into either the Box or Diamond defenses, one of the major defensive assets is that player adjustment is held to a minimum. Once the "denial" defender picks up his assignment, the full combination zone can easily be completed by shifting only a single player to fill the void (see Diagrams 6-22 and 6-23). In a somewhat corresponding manner, the shift from the "bottle" into the match-up triangle system again results in an automatic match-up system.

Assuming an excellent scouting report exists on a team which has roughly the same caliber personnel as ours, we usually begin the game with a tough man-to-man defense. The "denial" responsibilities are thus already matched up. Accordingly, if two players are to assume single-coverage, the man-to-combination shift also will result in an automatic match-up triangle zone combination.

With the current emphasis centering around two of the more innovative offensive formations—Passing Game and 1:4—we have continually searched for the best appraoch to counter these offenses. The Passing Game naturally requires more thorough pre-game scouting information because of its numerous variations and initial alignments. However, it can be adequately contained by assigning single-coverage to one of the two inside players and one of the three perimeter players. To counter the five-man Passing Game rotation, our method of attack is to construct an interior match-up triangle and man the two better perimeter shooters.

Against the standard movement of the 1:4 offense, we will match up with a passive man-to-man defense until we deem it necessary to shift into the match-up triangle, Box or Diamond depending upon the interior foot patterns of the two post men. Diagram 6-24 illustrates the coverage of the triangle once the shift from the man-to-man has taken place. Note that X_1 goes through with the point man as he passes to the outside and cuts to the corner. This particular shifting pattern is executed because of the nature of the offensive movement, whereby the opposite outside man comes out front for the reversal leading directly into the Shuffle, once the two inside players interchange. We also will assign single-coverage to the better shooter of the inside men (0_5). The second "denial" assignment is accorded the player guarding their best percentage outside shooter, 0_2.

There is endless planning which goes into constructing an intricate and varied game plan including a continuous multiple defensive attack. As the sophistication level of the total defensive system increases, it thus enables the coaching staff to refine its game-by-game approach. The ability to shift in and out of the more common active and passive defensive sets, match-ups and combinations in a transitional manner definitely boosts the possibilities of victory. When these various defensive maneuvers are sequentially organized to counter and re-counter the opposition, they can easily wipe out a majority of advantages that seemingly exist at the offensive end of the court.

When employing this type of pseudo-defensive philosophy to conceal either the match-up or the combination, one rule of thumb

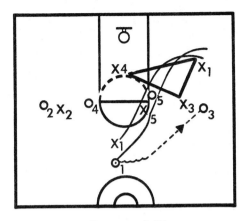

Diagram 6-24

stands out: *the longer a team is able to remain with its original defensive formation, the chances of keeping the opponent off-guard, once the combination shift has been executed, are measurably increased.* Just how long to stay with a particular defense is the single most ticklish problem which confronts the coaching staff. We attempt to get as much time from each defensive tactic as possible without reaching the point of diminishing returns. Therefore, our basic philosophy is to *stick with a particular defense until it shows signs of weakening, not until it actually does break down!*

As the defense noticeably shows the first signs of weakness, it is time to start anew with another of the conventional defenses and proceed to the necessary match-up and combination(s). By so doing you are not only regrouping your defensive forces, but also placing different pressure emphasis on the opposition. If a team has a variety of these defensive weapons at its disposal, the offense can never become fully comfortable with their attack since they must constantly alert themselves for another match-up or combination to be thrown at them at any time. This is the greatest tribute any defense-oriented team can attain . . . team intimidation.

CHAPTER 7

Complementing the Combination System with Pressure

In the modern game of power basketball, complete reliance on goal defenses is simply not enough to successfully counter the offensive attack over the course of an entire ball game. Regardless of the endless defensive variations, match-ups, and combinations used to shut off the scoring area, the truly outstanding defensive teams also possess the ability to extend their sphere of pressure emphasis far into the back court of the opponent. In our system of play, *back-court pressure is designed to aid the goal defense, not replace it!* Therefore, the press, or more properly, the existence of a press at either the three-quarter or full-court level is applied for a specific purpose within the spectrum of our overall game plan. *We never press just to be pressing and we seldom press for prolonged periods of time.*

Whenever we confront the opposition with a back-court press, it is to fulfill one of the following demands:

1. When we are behind and need to steal or intercept the ball by trapping it in the opponent's back-court area. This can also serve to speed up play when we need it.

2. Whenever we can exploit an individual or team weakness. *e.g.,* a team with only one ballhandler or a poor passing team.

3. To pit our superior conditioning and patience factor with that of our opponent.

4. To add another dimension to our defensive attack which
the opposition must consider in his game plan.

As noted at the outset of each of the chapters on the combinations, defenses are not permanently established for the whole game.
This same philosophy applies to the use of pressure in the back court.
We do not press for long periods of time because I am firmly convinced that a variance of pressure is far better than an extension of
pressure. Quick thrusts of full- and three-quarter court pressure, using
a variety of defensive fronts and trapping sequences, will be more in
line with the above-stated press rationale. By following this method of
pressure application, we have been less vulnerable to press-attack patterns. The team that presses from the opening whistle will soon be
forced out of its press formation because the offensive team, after
seeing the same press more than twice, can shift their attack away from
the areas of greatest pressure/trapping intensity. Thus, the press will
become a detriment as its effectiveness is gradually lost. This situation
becomes even more pronounced when the defensive team is obligated
to rely upon back-court pressure during the late stages of the game,
they will find themselves in serious trouble if they insist on relying on
the same press to get them back in the ball game.

Naturally, the type of back-court pressure we choose to place
on our opponent will vary not only from game-to-game, but from
possession-to-possession. We generally assume that our scouting report will supply us with the necessary information we can best use
against the opposition. Once this is done, it is up to the coaching staff
to decide whether we can afford to devote valuable practice time to
develop a back-court pressing defense. Whenever we do press, we
want/expect it to be effective and also smooth in its transitional phase
while rotating from a full- or three-quarter court pressure defense to
that of a goal defense at the other end of the court. This is our foremost
consideration when planning any form of back-court pressure tactics.

How the structure of the press relates to the formation of the
goal defense is most significant. More will be said concerning this
point at the conclusion of the chapter when its relevance can be more
appreciated in view of the various pressing techniques we will explore.

Just as there are passive and active goal defenses, the same
philosophy can be applied to any of the combination and conventional
presses. This includes both appearance and intensity. For example,
after a field goal, we use a sagging three-quarter press and allow the

ball to be inbounded. We can also deny the intial inbounds pass. Thus, it is possible to control pressure intensity relative to the game situation. In almost all instances, following a made free throw, we will attempt to deny the inbounds pass and apply a variation of full-court pressure intensity.

We use three of the standard pressure defenses in the back-court area: 3:1:1 (1:2:1:1), 2:2:1, and the straight man-to-man. In conjunction with these we have employed three combination presses: Diamond, Box and the Triangle at both the three-quarter and full-court areas. These press variations are more than enough since they present a multitude of defensive fronts and trapping sequences for the opposition to cope with. One rule remains constant throughout our use of the combination presses; we never use any of the better rebounders as the single-assignment player since we must be assured that he will be able to make the transition quickly to the goal defense without any hesitation or confusion. Also standard in our system is that whenever we are to drop back into one of the combination goal defenses, we never use any of the half-court zone presses because of the time element involved with reference to the drop-back responsibilities. There is not sufficient time for the goal defense and single-coverage assignments to be met.

Personnel placement in the establishment of any press is extemely vital. Regardless of whether the press be standard or a combination-type, the arrangement of player personnel should remain constant with only minor exceptions for single-coverage. Our guidelines are as follows:

1. The smaller players who cover the exterior/perimeter areas in the goal area defense will be those who occupy the front(s) of the back-court press.

2. Our forwards and post players will assume the responsibility for our back line of pressure defense in the mid-court area.

By positioning the players accordingly we have assured ourselves of a reasonably smooth means of transition from the press-type defense to the goal-protection defense. Movement from the press areas to the goal areas is also measurably reduced for all players and therefore, they will not tire as quickly as if they had to go from endline to endline. As a result of this position arrangement, the players are only required to make one quick initial move into their back-court placement—usually amounting to two or three steps—and then rotate and float according to the movement of the ball until they actually drop into the specific goal defense. The process of dropping into the final phase of the defense will thus be both quicker and easier if the players know that they do not have to run the length of the court to get into position following the press. We do not condone the "scramble-and-recover" method of defensive shifting. Not only is this sloppy in appearance, but too often results in missed assignments. Only five or six retreating steps should enable the press defenders to assume their roles in the goal defense plan. This we have found feasible by following the above-mentioned procedures. Because of the intensity of both our press and the scoring-area defense we present, it is imperative to our success that our players conserve as many steps in transition as possible.

The second reason for setting the press defense in this manner stems from the fact that we have discovered that the speed of the more mobile/smaller players insures that the back-court traps will be properly made in almost every circumstance. Once the trap is made, chances for the steal and interception are good! *Speed is the physical essential, anticipation the mental in setting effective trapping sequences.* During the past few years our forwards and post players have not been quick enough to react to the trap and as a result, were not overly successful. The smaller players (guards) are more familiar with this area of the court and consequently feel more at ease here.

Defensive-area familiarity has a tremendous amount to do with the success of your total defensive game plan. An example of this is that the back-line players, by being forwards and postmen, are better at anticipating the pass into their zone area and, therefore, are able to make more interceptions than the guards would in this area. The bigger players play in the "pass-and-score" area on the offense and goal defense and it is only logical that their experience in this realm be put to use on the press. Without question, this placement concept makes the job of teaching back-court pressure tactics to the team a much simpler task in the long run.

CONVENTIONAL PRESSES USED WITH THE COMBINATIONS

There is no doubt that all the standard presses, both zone and man-to-man, can effectively be used to complement the combination goal defenses. After years of careful scrutiny, there are only a few of these conventional pressing tactics which seemingly do a more thorough job of working harmoniously with the combinations in the scoring areas than others. For maximum press-to-combination transition results, there is no substitute for the trapping man-to-man, full- or ¾-court press. However, realistically speaking, this form of pressure quickly tires personnel, regardless of their conditioning and frequently results in momentary let-downs at the goal defense area. Depending upon the game situation, we will press with a zone-type variation 65 percent of the time. Thus, our attention has primarily focused on the zone press and its multi-frontal approach to back-court pressure.

There is a brief chart analysis of the two specific zone presses we use and their transitional relation to the combination goal defenses we most frequently employ on page 151.

It is not necessary to carry this analysis any further since the other odd and even front zone presses shift and rotate in a like manner once the initial inbounds pass has been made.

The principle of "keeping it simple" which we dealt with in several of the earlier chapters applies here as well. In Chapter 6 we noted that we do not always shift through a match-up phase in setting the goal defense for a variety of reasons, yet the majority of goal defenses we use are those which involve combination principles. This is true whether we press or not! Thus, whenever we choose to apply back-court pressure, in any of the more conventional forms, we will attempt to match its structure with that of the combination goal defense. The basic concept of "frontal consistency" must be continually kept in mind by our players when running both the press and combination goal defense. Single-front press implies a single-front goal combination; double-front press drops into a double-front combination and; man-to-man pressure implies shifting into the triangle. These "rules" are simple enough so that even the less-experienced players can understand them when they are reviewed at each practice session.

The Box and Diamond zones present few problems in dropping into their goal defensive arrangements when compared with those of the triangle zones. We have settled on the supposition that the more conventional zone pressure techniques do not lend themselves adequately to the triangle drop-back transitions. Taking two men out of the press as it reaches mid-court reduces the effectiveness of the press to

PRESS	GOAL COMBINATION	RATIONALE

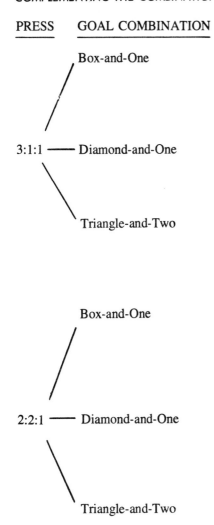

Box-and-One

Good. Rotation of the deep defenders provides for sound goal coverage positioning. Only possible problem here is that involving the "denial" assignment.

3:1:1 ——— Diamond-and-One

Excellent! The rotation lends itself perfectly to the drop-back positioning of the Diamond defenders (Diagram 7-1).

Triangle-and-Two

Poor. Too much confusion in picking up the single-coverage assignments in the goal area. Requires going through a match-up defense before setting the combinations.

Box-and-One

When single-coverage is concentrated on one of the offense's big men, this press is superb! The drop-back rotation is perfectly matched to this goal defense (Diagram 7-2).

2:2:1 ——— Diamond-and-One

Good. Because of the initial set in the back-court with a two-man front, there is the risk of possible confusion in setting the goal defensive front.

Triangle-and-Two

Not practical for the same reasons mentioned in the above 3:1:1 zone press.

the point of nullification! The two "denial" defenders know that their prime concern is attacking their specific assignments at the goal end of the court and they will be more intent on this than their zone press responsibilities—or at least they should be—in most cases. You can get by if only one of the players (when using the Box or Diamond) is anticipating his goal defensive challenge in this manner, but there is no

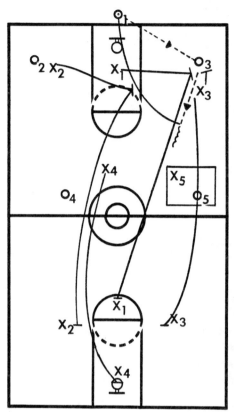

Diagram 7-1

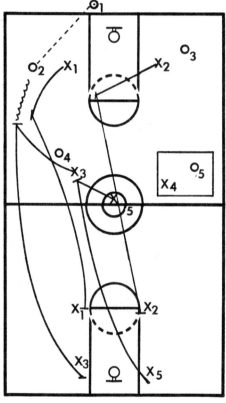

Diagram 7-2

hope for an effective zone press if two players share this same intense desire.

Therefore, when we are using the triangle zone series as the basic framework of our goal defense, we must rely on trapping man-to-man, back-court pressure. By so doing, the "denial" match-ups can be assumed immediately and the possibility of confusion is lessened once we cross into the opponent's scoring area of the court (Diagram 7-3). This has proved most effective in disguising the triangle goal defense, because we always use the match-up triangle and the opposition usually continues to read the defense as the straight man-to-man for some time.

Perhaps the greatest weapon we possess in running our defense evolves around using the press to rotate our defenses both in the front and back-court areas. By maintaining the concept of "frontal consistency," we are able easily to alter our goal defense by altering the front

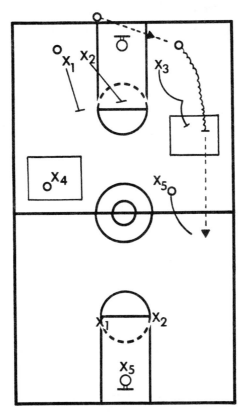

Diagram 7-3

of our press patterns. This can be done simply after (during) the foul shot lineup by a quick huddle, with the floor captain calling the shift. Also, while running the offense, a verbal command from the bench can accomplish the same thing.

In one such tournament game this season, we were working on the technique of altering our defenses according to certain keys. Prior to the opening tip for the start of the second quarter of play, I instructed the players that we were going to use the combination goal defenses for the entire quarter. Since we were already in the bonus free-throw situation, it would be up to the floor captain to huddle the team at the foul circle and call the press. For the first few press situations, I relayed press fronts to the floor captain. We began with a man press on the first-made set of free throws, thus dropping into a Triangle goal defense. On the second and third free throws, we used the 2:2:1 and a 3:1:1, showing the Box and Diamond combinations at the goal end of the court. The remainder of the calls were left to the discretion of the floor captain to vary as he saw fit. This system worked well enough to hold the opposition to four points, while enabling us to score 19—more than enough to pull away and win easily over a team that on paper looked to beat us badly.

COMBINATION PRESSES

From a coaching standpoint, this is one of the most fascinating aspects of modern basketball. Coach Al McGuire, of Marquette University, must be credited with bringing this to the attention of the nation's coaches. This is, indeed, one of the more exploratory phases of the game and an area where much new and innovative thought must be concentrated in the future. The majority of the combination press defenses noted in the following section are experimental and some still exist only on the drawing board. Hopefully, this brief discussion of some of the combination presses, along with the clinical discussions of Coach McGuire, will kindle sufficient interest among the nation's coaches where we will soon see more of these working models in practice.

Seldom has a sound combination press system been developed for use at both the college and high school level. Combining the best elements of man-to-man and zone coverage is a known commodity as far as goal defenses are concerned. However, this element should also be able to be successfully applied at the full- and ¾-court areas. Simple logic is the basis for this statement: *if the combinations are able to thwart offensive execution in the front court, so must they be able to achieve similar results when initiated somewhere on the court.*

All teams have specific, ruled-attacks for breaking both zone and man-to-man presses. When compared with the offensive continuity patterns, which are directed at the goal, these press-attack patterns are much more structured in nature. Whereas the offensive continuity always provides for the free-lance maneuver out of the pattern, press-attacks are not only governed by more rigid pass and foot patterns, but also must contend with the ten-second count. Against the better pressing teams, there is little free-lance back-court play that succeeds on an individual level—it takes a total team effort to break the good press. The only free-lance tactic that is encouraged is that of the clever ballhandler and he, of course, can be countered by the trapping methods of all presses.

Once again, the objectives of the press must be carefully defined as to whether it will be one of the ball-hawking variety or an exercise in mental and physical endurance. Combination presses are designed for applying maximum pressure on the ball in anticipation of causing the turnover. This is not to be taken as a desperation tactic, but a highly-controlled attack based on the same fundamentals as the various goal defenses.

A final point to consider regarding the employment of the combination presses, is how they will mesh into the total defensive picture. Are they easily and smoothly transitional into the standard, match-up, or combination goal defenses at the opposite end of the court? Can this be done quickly? There is nothing more awkward-looking and susceptible to the easy score than a team that is unable to convert the defensive transition.

Four-man Combination Presses: Box and Diamond

There are two approaches to the four-man zone combination press system. Perhaps these should more correctly be called options, since they are diametrically distinctive in virtually all aspects of operation. They involve the following:

1. The single-coverage defender can assume his role on the opponent's best ballhandler in back court and contain him until the ball crosses the ten-second line.

2. The concept of single-coverage on an assigned player is disregarded and the player not in the zone press formation serves as a "floater"—filler and trapper—within the confines of the Box and Diamond presses.

Examination of the rationale behind the employment of the four-man combination presses centers around the fact that the high-scoring continuity play in and around the goal area is usually directed by a single guard. Most of the post- and forward-oriented offenses do not, or more properly will not, sacrifice power for clever ballhandlers and thus there is need for only one guard in the rotation. As a result of this circumstantial alteration in today's game, many of the high-powered offensive teams are vulnerable to full- and ¾-pressure tactics. This is especially true if the lone ballhandler is so thoroughly covered that he cannot handle the ball in the back court.

Once the team ballhandler is eliminated from controlling the flow of action in the back court, the success or failure of breaking the zone press falls to the remaining players. Back-court offensive play is totally different from front-court (goal) play and the larger, less mobile, power players—those used to taking the ball and with one dribble, thrusting themselves toward the basket—are not as adept at handling the ball so far from the basket against pressure. This suddenly becomes a new and unfamiliar experience for these players. When compared with the time in which the big men handle the ball in the continuity offensive rotation—two or three seconds—the handling of the ball in the back court seems almost endless.

When working on the elements of combination press theory, our bigger players found that they were taking many unnecessary chances with the pattern-press attack (counter) because they were uncomfortable handling the ball in this court position. Frustration, confusion as who to pass to and nervousness were the comments most frequently overheard when they described their feelings after being confronted with a press of this type.

These points alone were enough to convince us that the idea of developing some form of pressure involving the combination was valid. After making several adjustments, we found this to be not only physically possible, but also practical because of our personnel. From the standpoint of being predominantly a combination-oriented defensive basketball team in the first place, the implementation of such pressing tactics was not overly complex.

The sound combination press has similar effects on the offense's press-attack that the Box, Diamond and Triangle have on the patterned-offensive goal thrusts, with only one exception. A well-run combination press will definitely force the opposition to consider altering its personnel so that they are assured of advancing the ball into the front court. This has to have a negative effect on the offense since they can ill-afford to sacrifice their power goal thrust for any length of time with two ballhandlers in the continuity attack. Under normal conditions, the power-offensive teams will attack the goal defense with four players. Consequently, if one of their power performers is temporarily forced to the sidelines for fear that the team cannot counter the press with a single ballhandler, this will reduce the offensive pressure on the defense (offensive potential) by approximately 20 percent-25 percent, depending on the scoring capabilities of the player inserted to counter the combination pressure in back court.

The concept of employing "denial" defense in the back court is the same as for the front court. One particular characteristic that is most necessary for this type defense is QUICKNESS! There is no substitute for this quality. The offense's chief ballhandler cannot be allowed any contact with the ball under any circumstances! We want him completely isolated from the flow of the ball in the back court and totally out of the ballhandling picture; thus we assign our quickest player to guard this offensive player—using a continual frontal (ball-you-man) position.

If the single-coverage offensive player should get the ball by freeing himself off a screen or another method, he will find himself trapped immediately by one of the zone defenders along with the "denial" player who has recovered from the screen. Therefore, he is constantly under pressure in the back court and must now get rid of the ball to a teammate not as familiar with the practice of handling the ball in this area of the court.

The second approach to the combination presses, that of using a single player as the "floater" within the press, is probably the more practical of the two methods. This idea of a "floater" will be further explored in the following discussions of the Box and Diamond combination zone presses at the ¾-court area. After considerable experimentation with both methods, we are leaning more toward this technique, since it is easier for our players to respond to the goal defensive assignments once the ball is brought across the mid-court line.

"Box-and-One Combination Press"

Our primary aim in employing the Box-and-One combination trap press is either to gain possession of the ball by means of an intercepted pass out of the trap, or to impede the opposition from crossing the ten-second line. As with every press designed, in the theoretical sense this particular press cannot be beaten.

Keying the successful execution of the Box-and-One press depends, to a large degree, on the intensity of play demonstrated by the "floater"—X_5 in the following diagrams. His perception of his dualistic role of trapper and filler will serve to make or break this press! The major characteristic trait that this player must constantly demonstrate is a combination of shrewdness and intelligence in his shifting movement. There can be no wasted moves on his part—he must know full well what his role will be in every back-court situation. This seems as though it might be too much to ask of the high school player, but with careful selection and practice he will soon emerge. Other traits we search for in this player are:

An ability to "read" the offensive set and know where he must station himself so as to be most effective.

Overall quickness to cover the territory.

Good size—preferably 6'1" to 6'3" to enact the traps successfully. If he is to be the front trapper—one nearest his own goal—size is important in that he will be able to place additional pressure on the ball since it is more difficult to complete a forward pass over a taller opponent.

As far as personnel placement is concerned, the front-line defenders on the press are those individuals who will be playing the positions farthest from the basket in our goal defensive alignment. This is consistent with the press placement theory expressed at the outset of the chapter. Such placement serves to decrease the amount of actual floor space that each player is responsible to defend. Therefore, the sole responsibility of the front-line defenders is to thwart any and all attempts by the offense to inbounds the ball to the middle and generate the press attack from there—regardless of the fact that they will be getting help from the "floater."

Since we desire to place the opposition in a position where they are forced to use the lob pass to put the ball inbounds, we want the front-line defenders to play the outlet men by using a frontal, or ¾-around, defensive position (see Diagram 7-4). Any opponent fears the consistent use of the lob pass as a means of inbounding the ball in back court because of the high probability of interception and thus the inbounds player must be patient enough to wait until one of the players frees himself for the initial pass. Once again, the clock favors the pressing defense since the inbounds pass must be completed within five-seconds after the official signals the ball ready for play—usually automatic once the player standing out of bounds touches the ball. We continually attempt to sell our players on playing a tough five-second press defense by an incentive reward system.

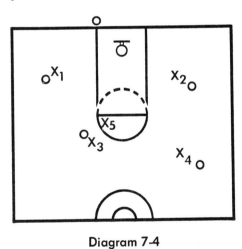

Diagram 7-4

Once the ball has been successfully inbounded, the role of the front-line defenders is analagous to that of the standard 2:2:1 zone press—guide the player with the ball toward the sideline until a trap can be made. We instruct our players to play the man with the ball ½-around during this phase of the press so that he will not be able to penetrate the middle of the court and thereby break the back of the

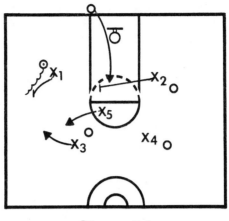

Diagram 7-5

press by dribbling. While this is taking place, the opposite front-line defender is responsible for filling the void toward the middle (Diagram 7-5).

Another noteworthy point regarding the positioning of personnel on the front line involves the fact that we always station our quickest front-line defender on the left side of the press. The thinking behind this is strictly one of percentage. By placing this defender here, we will usually force the ball to be put in play opposite this area—the outlet man in this area will be well covered so that he never gets the ball. Once we have forced the ball to be inbounded on the defensive right side of the court, we feel that we are in a commanding position in halting the opponent's press-attack because:

1. Since an overwhelming majority of players we face are right-handed, we attempt to force them to handle the ball with their weak hand. Most players are somewhat leary using the opposite hand in a tightly-congested or pressure situation. This fact is proportionally increased as you drop in skill levels from college to junior college and down to the high schools. If he is played tightly and intends to throw a forward pass, he must use either his left hand to direct the pass, or use a two-handed pass before the trap is executed. Once trapped, he has no alternative but to use his left hand to direct the pass out of pressure.

2. The area to be covered following the initial inbounds pass is sizable and requires a player who is super-quick to control both possible reverse or penetrating action here.

This adjustment on our part has had more to do with the success of our pressing teams than all the shifting techniques and rotations yet devised. Any coach who considers a pressing type defense for use during any or all of the season should sit down and jot down a list of all the teams he will face with good left-handed ballhandlers who can attack back-court pressure. Rest assured, probably less than ⅓ to ¼ of your league opponents have such a person. This, then, is a point you must exploit if you hope to gain an edge over the opposition.

The first duty of the back-line defenders (X_3 and X_4) is to match up with the offensive players in their specific area. In other words, we play a tight man-to-man with zone principles! These players must overplay the man in their area in a position we refer to as "ball-side around." (Diagram 7-6) This positioning forces the ballhandler deep in the back-court to throw the ever-tempting long lob pass down court—a pass that has an extremely low completion ratio.

Secondly, these back-line defenders must be able to rotate toward the trap situations with precision. This, like the goal transition mentioned earlier, must be a smooth, instinctive reaction. Constant communication among all the players involved with the press is an absolute necessity. Good floor communication will aid the back-line rotation to fill the voids as the frontal traps are enacted.

Our power-forwards and post men do the best job with this assignment partly as a result of default (we do not want them up front in the first place) and also because of instinct. Sticking with the philosophy of player consistency, these players are more familiar with the principle of hedging toward the ball because of their goal defensive tasks and also their positions which they assume at the offensive end of the court (constantly moving to the ball). These two elements, plus the previously-mentioned fact that they must play the deep spots on the goal defense, make them the logical players to defend this area.

A good measure of the fundamental strengths of any zone or man-to-man press is how well it protects the seams once the trap has been made. Any team can organize a trap anywhere on the court, but filling the voids and covering the potential receivers are not so easily

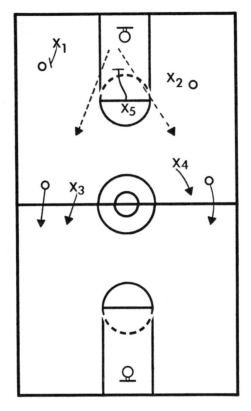

Diagram 7-6

accomplished. In the following diagrams (7-7 and 7-8) this factor is well noted.

Two items should first be mentioned about our concept of the trap, whether out of a combination or standard-type press:

1. If a team beats our initial trap with a penetrating pass we will drop to the goal defense immediately. Never will we attempt to trap again until we have had time to modify our method of filling the voids.

2. Whenever a team reverses the ball out of the back-court trap, they are indicating they cannot attack the press in a positive manner and we go after them with more intensity than ever.

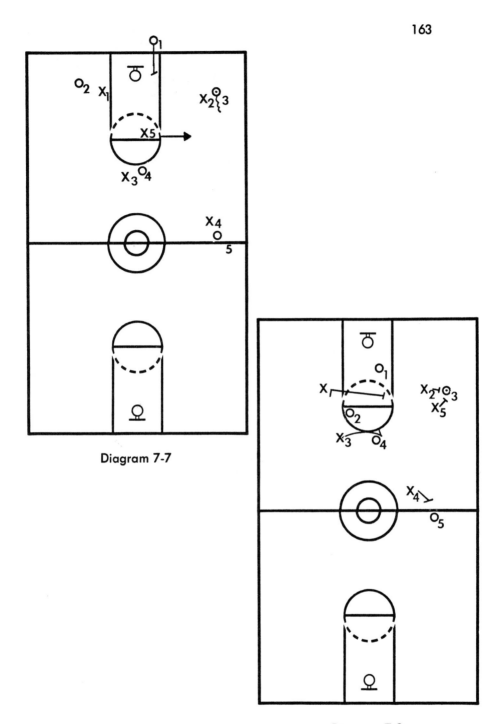

Diagram 7-7

Diagram 7-8

In the trapping philosophy of the Box press, X_5 is designated as the "floater" where he must not only perform traps on the sideline, but also fill the seams when he is not directly involved in the trapping action. Diagram 7-7 illustrates the defensive set after the ball has been forced to be inbounded to the right-hand side of the court—consistent with the pressure emphasis stated earlier. As O_3 commences the drive up the sideline, the "floater" assumes his role as trapper. X_5 does not begin to move to the ball until the initial dribble is made toward the sideline. Diagram 7-8 depicts the zone rotation once the trap is made. X_1 slides into a defensive position to intercept a possible pass out of the trap to either O_1 or O_2. X_3 and X_4 shift their zone areas in accordance with the movements of the offensive penetration. These players must not allow themselves to be beat deep, and at the same time, encourage the offense to throw the deep lob pass to the men in their area. A ticklish assignment for any defensive player, regardless of the skill he might possess! With practice, the players will eventually learn some of the "tricks" to covering this area.

Diagram 7-9 shows the zone shift to counter the reversal wherein X_5 now assumes his role as the filler. The back-line rotation, along with that of the opposite front-line defender remains consistent with the concept of plugging the holes in the middle of the floor while not permitting the completion of the deep lob pass. The final diagram concerning the Box press, 7-10, notes how this press combats the familiar inbounding tactic—the interchange. All the shifting practices hitherto discussed apply. Here, the "floater" quickly moves up to cut off the inbounds pass in the middle, while X_4 (playing the deep defender on the side of the interchange) fills the seam vacated by X_5.

"Diamond-and-One Press"

Whenever we use the Diamond-and-One combination press we allow the ball to be inbounded without an over-abundance of pressure on the opposition's outlet men. Depending upon the press-attack formation employed by the offense, we will station the point defender above or below the free-throw line, in a position to "guide" the inbounds pass. Also, in accordance with our front-line press philosophy, we always attempt to encourage the inbounds pass to come into the court on the right-hand side of the court (defender's right).

Personnel qualifications for the point position on the Diamond press are essentially the same as those for any of the various one-man

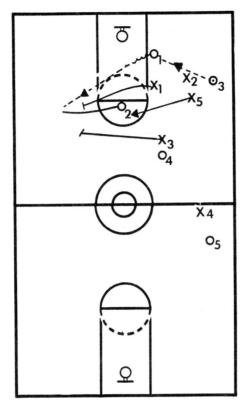

Diagram 7-9

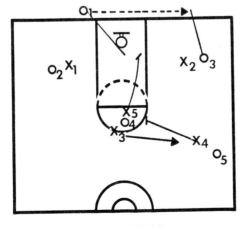

Diagram 7-10

front zone presses—quickness afoot and sufficient cleverness to force the ball to be inbounded to our preference side of the court. His speed will be one of the vital necessities when trapping. The "floater" (X_5) assumes either the role of a filler or takes up single-coverage on the opponent's best ballhandler in the zone press system. He is seldom involved in the direct trapping sequences unless his man gets the ball in the back court. His task immediately changes when he becomes the "floater" as noted in Diagram 7-11 when he confronts the reversal.

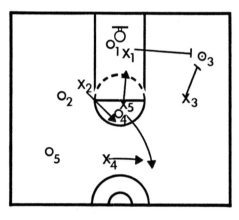

Diagram 7-11

Here, both X_2 and X_4 must station themselves in the passing lanes to prevent the foreward pass to either 0_4 or 0_5 down-court. The reversal to 0_1 is allowable in this press system since it is both time-consuming and involves virtually no penetration of the zone. Diagram 7-12 shows the rotation of the zone defenders with the possibility of a second trap when such a reversal occurs.

The deep rotation movement of X_4 (it is assumed that the post or one of the top rebounding forwards will be assigned this position) is vital to the success of the Diamond press. If he is not mobile enough to protect against the long passes or cannot react quickly to counter the reversal, the possibility of executing a second trap in the back-court is greatly diminished. This secondary trap is not mandaotry and need not even be considered unless a measurable degree of confidence in the movement of the deep rotation man exists in the minds of his fellow players. Once they know that their back line is well protected, the intensity of back-court pressure can be magnified.

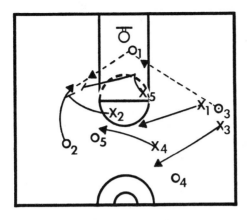

Diagram 7-12

Once again, depending on the single-coverage assignment, the two wing defenders will usually consist of those players who are our better trappers and fillers. They, too, must be mobile enough to make the rotation shifts away from the ball. This is, of course, the ideal situation and does not always present itself under actual game situations. One of the major advantages of this type of press is that there is a place—the wings—where one can put a weaker defender and still apply back-court pressure. With enough time and practice concentration, any average defensive player can be taught the wing-trap and wing-fill segments of the Diamond press.

"Triangle Combination Press Theory"

Operating the triangle zone press in the combination form involves three guiding principles:

1. No pressure is exerted directly on the player making the inbounds pass.

2. Trapping with this press set usually involves one of the zone defenders and one of the single-coverage players.

3. One of the single-coverage players will always cover the opponent's best ballhandler.

These are by no means the only rules for operation; rather they are the ones which we have been most attracted to during the past several seasons. This is by far the most complex of the combination presses to teach and put into use as part of the total press repertoire.

Since we match up our triangle press in the same manner as our goal defense, the triangle press can represent both a one- or two-man zone front (see Diagrams 7-13 and 7-14). There are many ways in which this press tactic could be employed, but it has proved most effective for us when the two single-coverage defenders are on both the deepest offensive player in the press-attack and the chief ballhandler—X_4 and X_5's duty in the diagrams above. Diagram 7-15 exemplifies the triangle encouraging O_3 to drive with the ball into a potential trap by X_1 and X_3, X_1's original position is in front of the offensive player in this area while X_2 is approximately 10-12' away (on a board-to-board basis) and in a position to intercept the inbounds lob pass. Again, we force this pass to the defensive right!

All traps out of the triangle press are to be those of the sideline variety; thus it is the task of the two zone defenders to execute the trap in this particular instance. As mentioned earlier, the majority of the trapping maneuvers will not involve two zone defenders but one of the single-coverage players and a member of the zone. For this reason, the prime function of the zone is to shift to fill the voids/gaps which the opposition will attempt to attack. The sideline trap is the main element of this press variation and when it cannot be enacted prior to the ball crossing the 21-foot line extended, the press defenders will retreat quickly to their prescribed goal defense responsibilities.

Secondary traps in the back court stemming from the reversals are to be used with extreme caution! There is too much risk involved in rotating the triangle more than once in the opponent's back court. It would seem that since this zone involves only three players it would be easier to shift than the four and five-man presses. This is true, since the rotation is simpler, but there is much more area for the offense to exploit.

We have had only limited success with this form of combination pressure because we expected too much from our frontal single-coverage player in the way of overplays. By having him slack off his assignment after the ball has been inbounded, he can devote more time to his role as a filler within the zone press and thus strengthen it. His prime responsibility remains the best ballhandler. However, if he can maintain a "ball-you-man" position inside the zone, this additional pressure can be intensified.

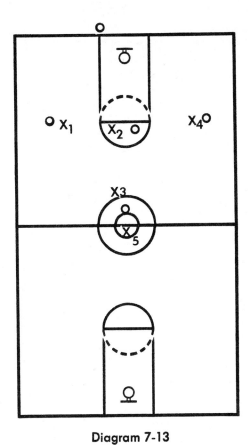

Diagram 7-13

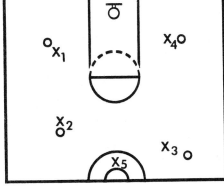

Diagram 7-14

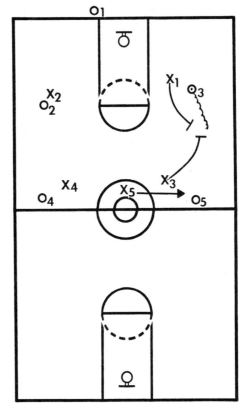

Diagram 7-15

THOUGHTS ON PRESS-TO-GOAL TRANSITION

Much has been written and said concerning the fluid motion of the transition from the press to the goal defenses. This single feature produces a cohesive effect, binding and linking the defensive maneuvers together. All transitions must be both simply accomplished and quickly/instinctively performed. *Minimum player movement is the key to success!* One of the old wives' tales that still avails itself whenever coaches get together states that "when a team uses a zone press, they must also drop back into a zone goal defense." This was a hard-and-fast rule for a number of years, until former U.C.L.A. coach John Wooden—during the dynasty years of the mid 1960's and

'70's—included several man-to-man principles which allowed his teams to retreat easily into their traditional tough man goal defense. With the evolution of game theory, this practice is now commonplace at both the high school and college levels. The hard core of the coaching profession are still of the opinion that both the zone-to-zone and man-to-zone transitions are by far the simplest types of transitional defensive technique to teach. Thus, this is what we see most frequently.

The emphasis of our pressing defenses with relation to the goal drops also centers around many complementary factors, not necessarily those which are identical. It is our feeling that *familiarity breeds perfection!* As an example, personnel placements on the press must be similar—at least in shifting technique—to that of their goal defense positioning.

Furthermore, it is also easier to shift from a combination press to a standard defense as well as from a standard press to a combination goal defense. In both instances, overall smoothness and drop-back rotation are assured since the assignments are relatively fixed.

When you are using one of the combination presses in the back court and need to employ a combination goal defense to stop the opposition, the defensive goal set should be initiated by first dropping into one of the conventional zone match-ups and proceed (as outlined in Chapter 6) from there. We follow this line of thought because if this method is not adhered to, the single-coverage assignments are temporarily left up in the air. A good defensive transitional team allows no time lapses. After all, super players will need only a split second to score, and therefore all preparation has gone for naught. In lieu of further explanation, note the shifting transition in the following diagrams (7-16 and 7-17).

Diagram 7-16 depicts the Box-and-One press trap broken along the sideline and the transitional drop-back movement. This team possesses a fine outside shooting guard (O_1) and also is stronger on the boards than we are. Therefore, we must drop back into a strong interior zone which can also contest the shooting talents of O_1—2:1:2. Our concluding shift from the conventional zone is to a Box-and-One to best counter the opponent's strengths. Diagram 7-17 shows the completed transition with X_2 taking the "denial" coverage on O_1 in the sequential shifting pattern noted in Chapter 6. X_2 takes O_1 after his initial possesion and pass. X_1 assumes this position on the two-man

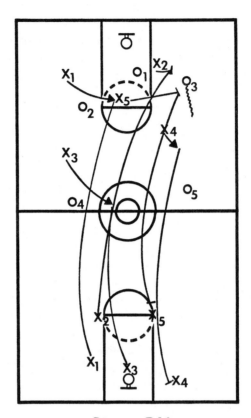

Diagram 7-16

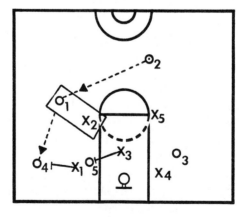

Diagram 7-17

combination front because of his size—usually he is a smaller player. X_3 slides to cover X_2's vacated baseline position.

These diagrams illustrate the close adherence to the ''rules'' regarding simplicity and minimal player movement. Similar cases can be made for all the other combination-to-match-up-to-combination transitional play. Naturally, this phase of the game needs to receive constant attention. When practicing this segment of our defense, I have found that our most meaningful drill involves setting the players in a back-court trap position, as in Diagram 7-15. We then remove the ball from the playing area and have a manager hold it above his head. As it is dropped, the defense must retreat to their respective goal sets prior to the third bounce of the basketball. This takes only about five minutes per day until it eventually becomes second nature. Not only has this increased our transitional speed after the opponent breaks our press, it has also greatly increased the speed by which all our defensive transitions take place.

CHAPTER 8

Rebounding and Breaking
from the Combinations

In accordance with our defensive game play, it is mandatory that the pressure philosophy framework remain intact while making the transition from defense to offense. Whenever a change in possession occurs, continuing degrees of pressure emphasis must be applied wherever this can be done most advantageously. This happens whether the change in possession transpires as the result of a pass interception, rebound, jump ball or, in some instances, after a score. *A break, in any form, is only as effective as the overall threat it creates!* We want our opponent to believe that we will utilize the break on every possession and in order to instill this "fear" in our opponent, we must be prepared to execute the break from anywhere on the court.

THE BREAK-THREAT CONCEPT

The break, of course, is only one phase of the total pressure plan, but it definitely allows the defense to continue its dominance over the game situation. This is primarily true because it is the defense which accounts for 80 percent to 90 percent of the break opportunities—from the missed field goal and free-throw attempts as well as the numerous turnovers it forces. Challenging the opposition to "beat the defense" at both ends of the court is our prime intent!

Under the rules of our pressure offensive system, for any break

174

to present itself there must exist a distinct numerical superiority factor—4-on-3, 3-on-1, or 2-on-1. Thus, the use of the break threat is essentially another variance of pressure application and change-of-pace action with which the opponent is forced to contend. Any team that is able to apply varying pressure tactics continually with both its offensive break threat and complementary defensive strategy has a better-than-average chance of creating scoring opportunities.

Labeling a break as fast, quick, etc. is somewhat misleading. Virtually all breaks that occur are both quick (in transition) and fast, but not all are planned or systematic. It is the *controlled break* and the continual threat of the break that truly supports our team's total attack. If the break can be advantageously put into practice, we take it; if not, we will simply pull back and get into our pattern offense, thereby forcing the opponent to defend our power attack—causing what we call "reverse pressure emphasis." This type of break formula is now quite commonplace among the major college powers. The poor concept of forcing the ball to the basket with a 2-on-2, or 3-on-3 situation is not encouraged unless the break involves our best one-on-one player, and even then, caution is the watchword. In most instances, this form of a forced attack does not complement our offensive philosophy of continuing strong pressure at all times. Such practice merely wastes an opportunity to lengthen the time by which we can apply offensive pressure to their defense. As indicated at the outset of this chapter, the break threat must be potentially strong enough to keep the opponent constantly off guard. Thus, our break rationale centers around the following:

1. The opposition must constantly be aware of the possibility of defensing the break with quick transitional movement from its offense to defense. This tends to make them more hesitant with their offensive attack. They must worry about always having a safety man in their offensive pattern to protect against the break.

2. It forces the opponent to carefully calculate the number of players they can send to the offensive boards. If the break threat can command sufficient respect that only three players are sent to the offensive boards, it will thereby nullify their "crashing power."

3. By and large, a team that executes the break well, will

seldom be pressed. There are times that we still encourage poor pressing teams to press after they score so that our press attack can be used to set up the break advantage. However, when we want to prevent our opponent from pressing us after a score, we employ a sideline break and get the ball to mid-court before their press can be set. (This concept will be noted in more detail at the conclusion of the chapter.)

4. When we run from the breaks which the defense offers, it gives our team members a definite pride in running the combination zone defenses. The break serves as a diversion from the intense hard-core defensive play we insist on at the opposite end of the court.

Numerous other reasons for running the break-threat patterns in a highly-controlled fashion can be extolled and their validity upheld. However, the above-listed rationale is sufficient justification for our employment of this type of break philosophy, since it is this form of percentage basketball upon which our system is based.

REBOUNDING PRINCIPLES FROM THE
THREE AND FOUR-MAN ZONES

It is a foregone conclusion that you must possess the basketball in order to operate any form of the break threat and the easiest means to gain possession of the ball is from rebounding the missed field goal attempt. The elements of sound rebounding are one of the most significant considerations in the construction of any defensive system. Such is the case with the combinations. For the running, breaking team, the rebound and outlet pass are the most important phases of the game.

There is no question that the well executed semi-zone (combination) will force the opponent to take a more pressurized shot at the basket than the more conventional defenses and, therefore, can anticipate a greater number of rebounding opportunities. Because the majority of our combination defenses are of the match-up variety, the interior and exterior defenders have a better-than-average chance of securing the carom from the boards since they are pitted against a specific player in an area and not against the area itself. This concept of specified rebounding assignments is one of the major reasons for utilizing the combination-match-up defenses in the first place. It is also a proved fact that most zone defensive teams surrender more offensive rebounds than either the straight man-to-man or combination teams because the blocking-out assignments are not individually designated, nor do they contain any real consistency.

Rebounding principles from both the combinations and straight zones must be stressed at every practice session during the course of the season. Several statistics reinforce this personal obsession. During the past four seasons, our opponents shot at a 38.5 percentage rate from the floor while taking an average 61 shots at the basket per game. This is further broken down into 22 made field goal attempts (16 from the initial attempt and 6 on follow-ups) and 39 total missed attempts that we could possibly command by means of defensive rebounding. We did not gain possession of the possible 45 misses (39 initial misses plus the 6 possible we surrendered) as the statistics indicate. However, we have found that when the number of our follow-up conversions is compared with that of our opponents, we have been statistically more effective in 85 percent of the games played. Although we are guilty of surrendering an average of 6 offensive rebound conversions per game, we have averaged 9 such scoring/follow-up rebounds against our opponents who used the more conventional defenses. When the number of total follow-up possessions which are not converted is tabulated, our advantage is also much greater. Thus, we seem to do a more consistent job of limiting the opposition to fewer follow-up scoring opportunities.

We believe that our players should retrieve between 67 percent to 70 percent of the defensive rebounds possible. Thus, if we apply a minimum 67-percent recovery factor to our defensive rebounding, it means that of the 45 actual missed field goal attempts, we ultimately should get possession of 30 rebounds. In addition to this, we usually get 8-10 defensive free-throw rebounds during the course of the contest. Certainly not all of these opportunities offer possibilities for a controlled break-threat situation. Depending on the style of play used by the opponent, the possible advantage break situations will range between 30 percent and 50 percent of the total possessions. As a general rule, the more patterned the offense, the lower the percentage of break situations.

Perhaps one of the most exhaustive and interesting clinic

speakers on rebounding is George Raveling, Washington State University coach. He cites numerous methods for defensive board control. Several of the significant points from coach Raveling's rebounding philosophy receive daily attention at our practices. Noted below are the following we drill on constantly:

1. When a shot is taken, *watch your man,* or when playing a zone or combination, the man in your area and *not the ball.*

2. *Make contact* with the offensive player and keep him on your back so he does not slip around toward the goal.

3. *Jump for the ball at an angle* and not in a straight-up direction—it is too easy to lose balance going straight up and down. A slight bump will move you out of good defensive rebound position.

4. Keep all players in constant *communication* with one another so that they are ready/alert to probable rebound situations. Call out the "shot" when taken.

Because of the adherence to these rules and fundamentals, we attempt to create a 1:1 rebounding ratio with our opponent when running the multiple defenses or combinations. Our communication and shifting techniques also enable us to prevent the offense from confusing the defensive assignments and thus our rebounding designations remain clear. Therefore, the possibility of error is thereby lessened considerably. Note the shot coverage and rebound-position afforded the various combinations in the diagrams below (8-1 through 8-3) versus the angle, corner/baseline and point shots. Diagram 8-1 shows the match-up rebounding responsibilities to be relatively simple from the Diamond, while 8-2 shows that even though the ball is headed for X_2's area, he must search for the man in his area, lest he slip around the defender and gain inside position for a possible tip-in. X_1 does not screen out the man in his area in this particular situation unless he is inside the free-throw line extended. This concept applies to both shoulder box defenders.

In order to check on the effectiveness of our team rebounding, we review each of the situations (Diagrams 8-1 to 8-3) daily. We attempt to control the offensive rebounder by gaining position on him so that the ball hits the floor twice before it is recovered. This simple check shows who is doing the job as far as the screening-out responsibilities are concerned.

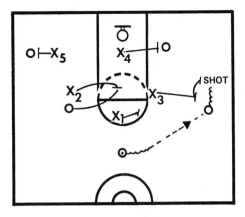

Diagram 8-1

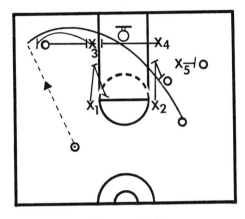

Diagram 8-2

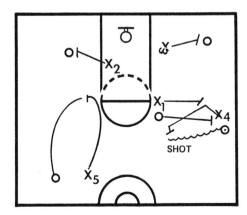

Diagram 8-3

OUTLET AND BREAK-THREAT ORGANIZATION

Obtaining possession of the basketball by getting the rebound is, obviously, only half the battle when beginning the actual break-threat movement. The ball must get to the right floor position at the proper time, with the floor quarterback having control. Although I do not feel that our break philosophy is radically different from most break teams, we assign specific players as the outlet receiver in virtually all instances. The idea of having an ''assigned-outlet'' man seems as though it would greatly impede the speed of the break. To a slight degree this is true, but whatever our break appears to lack in speed, it more than makes up for in security of execution. Once the ball is in the hands of the assigned outlet, we have found that we follow through the entire break-threat pattern with a great deal more organization.

The adoption of the single, or assigned-outlet system has several vital advantages:

> When all the players know who the assigned outlet is, the rebounders are never confused as to where the outlet pass should go. We have always had a problem with the rebound that is retrieved in the center position, as well as the board garnered by the forward who has already turned to the inside. Since we have gone to the assigned outlet system, these momentary lapses are non-existent. The consensus of opinion among our rebounders is that it is easier to look for a specific player than an area and a player before releasing the outlet pass.

> All the players know exactly where they belong on the break-threat pattern once the rebound has been secured and there seldom is duplication of players filling lanes or confusion as to who should fill what lane and who should be the ''trailer.''

Primarily because of these two points, the assigned-outlet system has worked well for us when we have had both the exceptional-and average-talent years. To be honest, the use of the single-outlet has worked best when our talent has been thinnest—something for the coaches with marginal talent to consider!

As noted in Chapters 2 and 3, the type of player we want for the top of the combination goal defense is the quick, heady ballhandler who can also lead the break. Aside from these requirements, this player must also possess the ability to free himself for the "board-to-board" pass from the rebounder, and be capable of moving the ball up-court in traffic until a player is open ahead to pass to. Along the way, there are a number of circumstances where he must make a decision to continue the break threat or terminate it. His split decision is all-important and it is for this reason, above all others, that great care goes into the selection of who the assigned outlet will be. We have been fortunate over the past two seasons to have more than one such player on the team and thus have been free to alternate this duty upon occasion. Furthermore, being a defensive-oriented basketball team, our responsibility in this area definitely supersedes our potential break alignment. However, we never waste an offensive break-threat opportunity since this is considered to be a defensive rest period and our players look forward to this brief interlude.

Our controlled break threat has four guiding fundamental concepts which must be strictly adhered to during its course of action. These "rules" remain intact whether the assigned-outlet player is one of the "denial" defenders or a member of the combination.

> *Rule #1*— Once the rebound is recovered, the assigned outlet *lines up with the ball on "board-to-board" basis*—in relation to the rebounder —approximately at the top of the key (21-foot line extended (see Diagram 8-4).

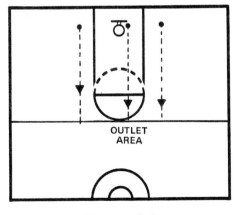

Diagram 8-4

Rule #2 — *Initiate the break from the ball-side.* If the ball is rebounded within the confines of the key area, it is to be brought down the middle lane of the court whenever possible. Consequently, if it is boarded beyond this area, it will preferably be brought down-court in the specified outside lane.

Rule #3 — *Move the ball ahead* to the nearest open man whenever possible! This can be somewhat misleading to younger players who do not know when and when not to advance the ball forward. However, what we want to avoid is over-dribbling on the part of the assigned-outlet man on the break attack.

Rule #4 — *Fill the proper lanes.* This is common break practice at the offensive end of the court. We insist that the break starting from the rebound be of the three- and four-man variety (using a "trailer"), thus forcing our players to use the odd-numbered lanes for their primary thrust and leaving the even-numbered lanes for the "trailer." From the quick break (intercepted pass) the rules are just the opposite in most cases. Diagram 8-5 illustrates the lane designation while the following diagram, 8-6, illustrates the complementary drill we use to practice lane occupancy.

The Circle Drill (8-6) is done with the coach or manager putting up a shot at the basket while the players continue in a circular motion around the free-throw line. Prior to the shot, a specific inbounds and outlet man is assigned. Once the shot is taken, the break threat is executed depending on whether the shot is made or not.

The majority of the above-mentioned "rules" are doctrinaire and warrant little explanation here. Perhaps the first rule (#1) regarding the positioning of the single outlet, merits some further discussion. Regardless of who is designated as the outlet, it is imperative that he be able to free himself adequately to receive this initial pass to set up the break. Merely racing to the proper reception spot is not always enough. In addition, this method does not always assure a good angle for

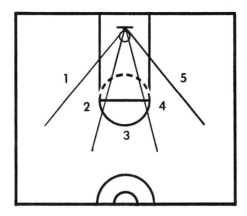

Diagram 8-5

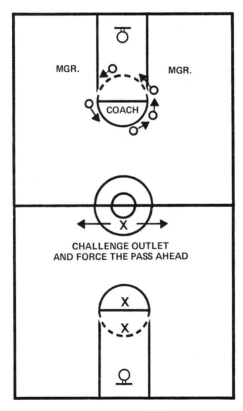

Diagram 8-6

reception of the outlet pass. The first pass on the break must be executed flawlessly, otherwise the actual threat will be lost. To insure the proper reception angle and also to provide for the outlet man to "shed" his defender, we insist he perform a quick V-cut to the ball (Diagram 8-7). This usually amounts to having the assigned outlet going to his position and taking one step toward the ball.

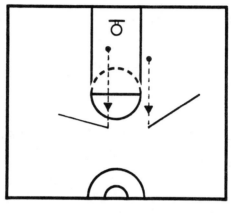

Diagram 8-7

Many coaches have discounted the philosophy brought about in Rule #2, although some of the major college powers, who once were strong advocates of the traditional "middle-lane" break, are now incorporating bits and pieces of this break ideology into their system. There surely is not a hard-and-fast rule that stipulates that the ball must be brought to the middle of the court at any time during the break. We use the middle lanes when open, but we find that being flexible and using the outside lanes when they are available to us is most beneficial because:

1. There is less chance of being blind-sided by a retreating opponent and having the ball knocked away from behind. Most players hustling back on defense will use the middle lanes to get into their goal defensive position.

2. The outside lanes, when properly run, offer a greater visibility spectrum for the ballhandler. He is better able to pick up both the remaining break players and also the cutters (trailers).

3. Because this break pattern is not commonplace, it is more difficult to defend since most teams prepare to stop the break from the standpoint that it originates from the middle lanes.

USING BOTH ZONE AND "DENIAL" PLAYERS AS THE ASSIGNED OUTLET

The use of the single-coverage player as the outlet is by far the simplest form of getting the ball to mid-court. Whenever we are fortunate enough that single coverage exists on a guard, a smooth transition from defense to offense (break attack) should materialize since the outlet assignment can be made virtually "automatic," depending on whom we signal out for "denial" coverage. If we feel that our defensive makeup will not be sacrificed and are able to run on our opponent, we will temporarily match up our best outlet guard to the opposition's star player. When employing the three-man zone combinations this match-up can usually be attained, but in the four-man zones this is not always so easily accomplished.

If single-coverage is to be handled by a forward, we will quite often designate him to be the assigned outlet, especially if he is a decent ballhandler. When we have decided to adopt this method of outletting the ball, we seldom permit this player more than one or two dribbles after he has received the initial pass. He is instructed to pass the ball ahead to one of the better ballhandlers almost immediately—to any such player in an odd-numbered lane. We would rather he not dribble the ball at all, but this is not entirely practical and if one has any apprehensions about a forward handling the ball in back court, I would suggest that he simply avoid falling into the trap of using the single-coverage player as the outlet. Diagram 8-8 denotes the use of the "denial" forward as the single outlet and the concept of quickly releasing the ball ahead from this position.

One rule we have is never to permit the post to serve as the assigned outlet. Furthermore, he is not to handle the ball in back court at any time, if it can be avoided. Regardless of whether he is involved with single-coverage or the semi-zone, it is a physical impossibility for this defensive player to consistently get into position quickly enough to receive the outlet pass. This rationale centers around the fact that he is required to remain low for rebounding purposes. In many situations the

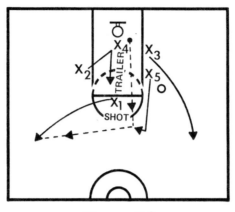

Diagram 8-8

same argument can be made for the forwards. Another very important reason for not using the post as the assigned outlet is that it would nullify his role in the actual break threat—as one of the power players attacking the basket on the move—because he would now have to assume the role as a secondary thrust player.

The practice of using one of the zone defenders as the assigned outlet is somewhat more difficult to execute as his zone shifting responsibilities are more demanding. There is little question that this player must work harder to get to the reception area because of his position within the zone or combination. Note the examples cited below using one of the zone defenders as the single outlet (Diagrams 8-9 through 8-12).

Since we have introduced this system, only one drawback aside from the previously mentioned speed factor has come about. With only one player handling the initial outlet pass, he will quickly be picked up by his defensive assignment, or prevented from getting the outlet pass from the rebounder. Many teams spend a great deal of time devising tactics to slow down breaking teams. On several occasions, we have found that we are forced into making adjustments in order to sustain the break threat. When facing a team that attempts to halt our single-outlet system, three distinct alternatives present themselves:

1. We can assign another player this duty on a temporary basis until he, too, is picked up by the alert defensive team.

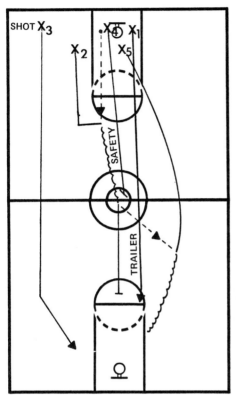

Diagram 8-9

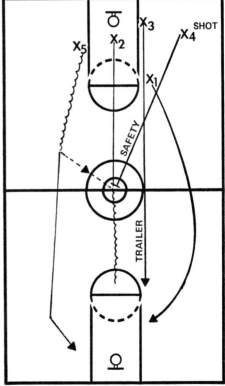

Diagram 8-10

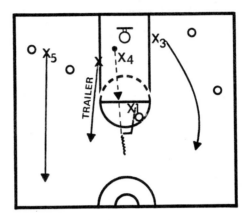

Diagram 8-11

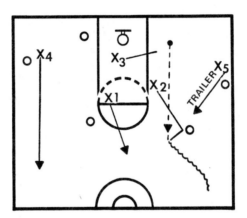

Diagram 8-12

2. On each possession, we can rotate the assigned outlet responsibility between two players on a coded key.

3. We can assign two outlet men and key their movement by whoever is nearest the floor (board-to-board) position to handle the pass.

Since practicality dictates most of the strategic decisions in the game of basketball, option number two in the above list must be ruled out immediately. The players in our system have enough things to concern themselves with during the course of the game, and adding such a rule would only serve to confuse matters. The third alternative is both practical and feasible, but there will always be a time when there are two men lined up for the same outlet pass. The possibility also exists in reverse when both players will release, thinking that it is the job of the other to handle the outlet and the rebounder is thus committed either to handling the ball himself or gambling on a long pass into the front-court. Quite obviously, this third option often results in hesitation—precisely what the slower break-threat team does not need!

Re-assignment of the outlet is therefore the most logical path to pursue when the defense places added pressure on the designated outlet man. It will usually take some time for the opponent to discern the breaking technique and when it becomes evident that he has, another player must assume the role of the assigned outlet. As a rule of thumb, we have sought to switch outlet men every quarter and this has virtually eliminated any semblance of serious defensive pressure from being successfully applied on the outlet man in the back court.

All teams have a type of "trailer" series at the conclusion of their rebound break. In this respect we are no exception. However, I am undoubtedly one of the few coaches who feels that we should not use the "trailer" series unless we really need such a direct thrust at the basket. The use and development of a sound concluding break attack is extremely relevant for a majority of the teams we face on the schedule, but we use it very seldom since *it does not sufficiently complement our pressure concept!* The basis for such a statement rests with the following:

> All "trailer" systems offer too tempting a situation to force the ball to the basket before a higher percentage shot avails itself.

> Our players work so intensely to exert pressure on the opposition's offensive players that they must be allowed to place full offensive pressure on the opposition's defense by attacking them with our continuity pattern.

> We cannot expect our players to play defense for more than 60 percent of the time just because they want to take the quick shot at the offensive end of the court. Regardless of the strength of the team defense, the coach cannot ask the players to play only defense!

Whenever we do use the "trailer" to conclude our break threat, the purpose for its employment is highly strategic. There are only three such instances when we want to include the "trailer" series in our break:

1. When we are behind and need the quick shot near the end of the half or in a definite catch-up situation.
2. When we desire to increase the tempo of the game.
3. During the opening moments of the game to establish the fact that we can score when we run.

"Trailer" patterns are as varied as continuity patterns—some very elaborate and others consisting of simple maneuvers. Because of the complex structure of our defense and dedication to a continuity offensive pattern, we allow a great deal of freedom (as a change of pace for the players) with the "trailer" series. Diagram 8-13 shows the simple approach to the break conclusion by the use of the 4-man

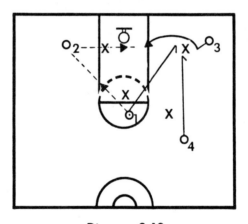

Diagram 8-13

passing-game movement whereby we pass and screen opposite the ball, looking for the open man. This has proved most effective for us thus far. The only stipulation that is built-in is that once the "trailer" series begins, only two passes are allowed. If we do not have a high-percentage shot after these two passes, we will drop back into the pattern continuity.

QUICK BREAKS FROM THE COMBINATIONS

The quick break emanates from an intercepted pass and is perhaps the only "pure" break our players run. By the term "pure," I mean free-lance. We feel that we should score off this type of break every time since the defensive players should not be able to halt our thrust at the basket. This method of break threat is also the best single means of applying reverse pressure on an offensive-oriented team. Most offensive-minded teams are those who are least prepared to handle the offensive thrust directed at them. In general, most teams do a poor job of defending the quick break (retreating defense) and are considerably more vulnerable than against the rebound break. We have found that our conversion rate from the quick break is almost triple that of the rebound break.

Conversely, because of our basic combination defensive philosophy, our players seem to handle the quick-break defense quite well—dropping into two- and three-man zones until full recovery is made. We have been able to stop our opponents from scoring over half the time! Not many teams can say this. I firmly believe that since our players are schooled in the player-area defense concept from the first day of practice, we thus concede fewer unmolested breaks. Many is the time we have had two players stop the opponent's thrust with three and four players.

Getting back to the quick break, it is only natural that we have taken some precautionary measure for its application. For any type of break to succeed there must be some guiding principles. Because we desire this to be done instantly, only two points need to be carefully heeded after the pass interception:

1. If the ball is intercepted/recovered below the foul line extended, we will use the assigned outlet to begin the break-threat action (Diagram 8-14).

2. When the ball is recovered beyond the foul line extended, we use the player who recovered the ball and the nearest player(s) to fill the break lanes.

A majority of the recoveries occurring beyond the free-throw line extended present a two-on-one opportunity. These, of course, are

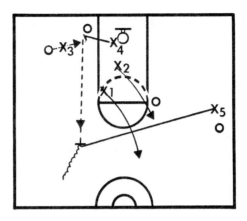

Diagram 8-14

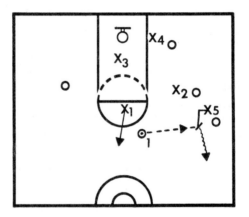

Diagram 8-15

the easiest breaks to convert and should be automatic. Diagram 8-15 shows the interception by X_1 and the potential quick break that ensues. X_1 and X_5 would be the two players involved, along with their defenders, yet a clear break should transpire here against the single defender—O_1. In this particular situation, as in all such two-on-one breaks, our players are encouraged to use the even-numbered lanes once they approach mid-court (refer to Diagram 8-5). Ideally, when operating the two-on-one break from the ¾-court area, we attempt to turn the head of the defender by using several crisp passes between the players involved. Once we get his attention focused on one player, this player drives until he is completely covered and then passes off for the easy lay-in.

There are coaches who profess that the more times the ball changes hands on the break, the lesser the chances for conversion. This is true for the most part, but in our two-on-one quick break, the "pass-pass" concept is almost second nature to our players since they use this Bob Cousy Drill series to open every day of practice. Therefore, this is simply a reflex action on their part and a thing of beauty to observe from the sidelines. Below are the two drills we use to complement this phase of our transitional attack (Diagram 8-16, pass-pass, and Diagrams 8-17 and 8-18 showing both ends of the 3-on-2, 2-on-1 continuation drill).

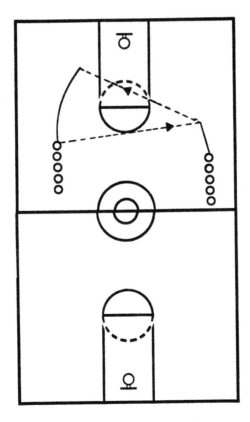

Diagram 8-16

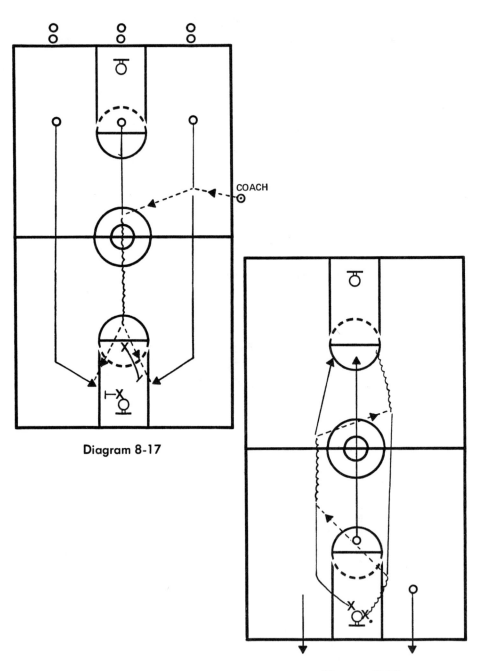

Diagram 8-17

Diagram 8-18

SIDELINE BREAKS FROM THE COMBINATIONS

The idea of continual pressure also applies to the split second after the opponent has scored. It is here that temporary lapses frequently provide easy access to the opponent's scoring area. He must be aware that if he does not react quickly we can, and will, break from this floor position. The sideline break threat is nothing new, but it does add another dimension to our total pressure attack. Our method of attack after the opponent has scored is also a very controlled break form—perhaps even more so than any of the breaks we run.

As with any break system, there are certain guidelines which accompany the execution of the sideline break pattern. Running this from the three-and four-man combination defenses is not much different from the more conventional defenses. We have run it several different ways, but the most organized form of the break has come about when we have followed the three principles listed below:

1. Zone defender nearest the basket when the field goal or free throw is made serves as the inbounds man to initiate the break threat.

2. Player responsible for the individual who scored becomes the outlet and goes to a position along the closest sideline, 21-feet out for the first pass—top of the key extended.

3. Zone defender who is farthest from the basket sprints to the same sideline as the second pass receiver in a position approximately 5 feet to 10 feet beyond the mid-court line. The pass should be there the same time the receiver gets there.

Our sideline break is only a ¾ variation and is used in the same vein as the rebound break threat. The same concept of bringing the ball down the outside lanes, looking for the open man ahead, remains consistent. Note the player movement in the following diagrams when the shot has been converted from the corner (Diagrams 8-19 through 8-21).

We run the sideline break after a score in this manner because the shifting of the combination zones provides for an unbalanced floor as the shot is released. This fact should be capitalized upon! Therefore,

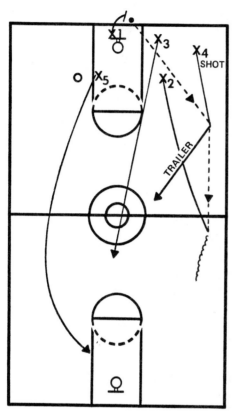

Diagram 8-19

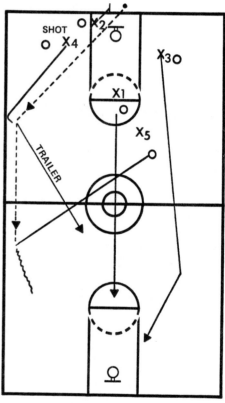

Diagram 8-20

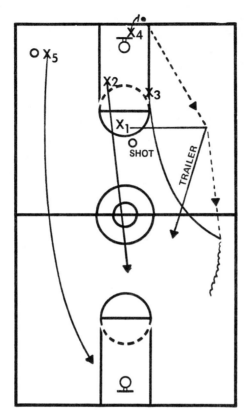

Diagram 8-21

it is only logical that the break be run on the over-loaded side of the floor. After the second pass, the ball is well beyond center court and will be dribbled into one of the odd-numbered break lanes while the other break players fill the necessary lane positions. Again, only if applicable do we ever attempt to run the "trailer" series on this possession.

Because the outlet responsibilities are different from the rebound break situations and need not be the same for any two possessions, it is very difficult for the defending team to set up its full-court press to halt our initial inbounds pass. The quickness with which the ball is moved into the opponent's front court makes the full and three-quarter presses nearly impossible to set. As *the basket is scored at one end of the court, we can be attacking the opposite basket with three men within three to four seconds*. This, then, is one of our most serious break threats which the opponent must consider!

Today's game is a fast-paced affair. More accurately, the style of the game at both the high school and college level requires that the players be able not only to play under different pressure variances, but also in a controlled manner. Playing under control with the numerous transitions from offense to defense is indeed difficult. As a result of this fact, the rules for execution of both the offense and defense must be as complementary as possible and also well-based in fundamental game theory. Knowing when, where, and how best to gain the advantage on your opponent lies deep in fundamental execution of your partiular philosophical approach to the game.

CHAPTER 9

Offensive Patterns that Complement the Combination Defenses

Basketball, more than any other sport, has been described as an exercise in total team pride. All of us involved in coaching the game know this to be an accurate assessment. Perhaps this element serves as the single-greatest incentive to all championship teams. Attempting to define pride in this framework is a virtual impossibility. However, there are two distinct phases in which this seemingly intangible factor can be brought into the scope of reality: offensive and defensive pride. We have referred to defensive pride as essentially the state where the various segments (players) surrender their individualism to achieve all-out team unity and intensity while playing without the basketball. Offensive pride consists of the manner in which the total team offensive skills are displayed when converting a score.

Although team defense wins games by presenting the offense with countless scoring opportunities from turnovers, steals, rebounds, etc., we constantly strive to impress on our players that it is the potency of our offensive continuity attack and its various options that puts the actual points on the scoreboard. Stolen passes, rebounds, jump-ball controls, *et al.*, do not count on the scoreboard and therefore it is up to each individual to assert enough self-pride to develop his offensive skills to the point where we can rely on him to confidently take the opposition's best defensive player one-on-one to the basket! Once a

199

player demonstrates this attitude and the corresponding skills to perform this movement, we hopefully conclude that he is ready to play the
offensive end of the court with the same tenacity in which he plays his
defensive role.

FORCING THE OPPONENT TO RESPECT
YOUR OFFENSIVE ATTACK

We must assume that whenever we step onto the playing court,
the opposition is 100 percent—mentally and physically—prepared to
play us. Any other supposition on our part (or on the part of any of our
players) would be foolhardy. Regardless of the fact that they are 100
percent prepared for us, a question exists as to whether they are sufficiently prepared for both our defensive and offensive plans. In a majority of our own instances, the opponent's preparedness factor has been
unequally divided into a 30-70 ratio: 30 percent devoted to stopping us
offensively, with the remaining 70 percent dedicated to exploiting us
defensively. This imbalance exists primarily because they will usually
be forced to cope with a multiple combination defensive attack with
varying degrees of pressure and, thus, they desire some form of assurance of being able to counter our defensive maneuvers. Therefore,
*whatever we can do to increase the opponent's defensive awareness
toward our offensive tactics will proportionately lessen his own offensive capacity!* Once the offense-oriented team begins thinking in terms
of defensing our offensive patterns they are playing a negative or
regressive brand of basketball. The more balanced (50-50) the percentage distribution becomes during the first few minutes of play, the
more effective our defensive ploys will be over an entire game.

Each team in our league knows full well that we are basically a
defensive-minded team and knows that their best chances of beating us
are to spread our defense with their continuity patterns while paying
only token attention to our offensive pattern play. Since we have not
been blessed with outstanding perimeter shooters during the past few
seasons, we have seen nothing but tight zones and sagging man defenses. Consequently, our players have become highly dedicated to a
diciplined effort while in our basic continuity attack.

Combining this personnel problem with size limitations, it has become our prime concern to *make the opponent work continually to defend our penetration toward the basket for the high-percentage shot.* It has been our feeling that we work hard on defense, so why shouldn't our opponent! This fact was earlier alluded to in Chapter 8 where it was mentioned that each of our offensive possessions was also considered a defensive rest-and-recovery period for our players. This is an important selling point to a defense-oriented team, but it cannot be allowed to be taken too literally, condoning any lapses in pattern execution. Player concentration must be just as keen at the offensive end of the court as it is at the defensive end, though not as physically aggressive.

When discussing our opponent for the next game, we are careful to assess whom and where our offensive thrust can and should attack. Every team, regardless of the caliber of its players, has an Achilles Heel! This philosophy enables us to place considerable pressure on a specific area or player, thereby forcing the opponent's defenders not directly involved with this attack to slack off their assignments and compensate for their teammates who are bearing the brunt of the offensive penetration. Any team that can direct its offensive thrust in this manner, while taking only high-percentage shots from the 10 to 15 foot range, will be more than competitive.

Several of the tactics we often employ early in the game to force the opponent to even out his pre-game preparation balance and play a more intense form of defense on us are:

1. *Turning over the continuity three or four times* before attempting a shot at the basket. By so doing, each player in the offensive rotation will be more familiar with the feel of the game ball and also the defense will be obligated to shift in several different directions in order to counter our overall pattern movement.

2. *Spreading the offense* and making the defense come out and play us tighter on the perimeters. This is not designed as a stall, but rather used as a means to get the opponent to over-extend his defensive set.

3. *Using the sideline and rebound break threat* to test the opposition's ability to switch from offense to defense and make them aware of our running game.

4. *Force the opponent to switch assignments.* These are usually fixed prior to the opening tipoff by the coach and

most teams do not like to switch early in the game for obvious reasons. In most cases, they prefer to fight through or over the screens. We have found that this can result in uncertainty and confusion on the part of the defensive team.

5. *Showing a new pattern* of one or two moves—perhaps just an initial move or two to get into the offense—in order that they might have some problems with their early match-ups. If this is successful, they will usually be forced to call an early time-out to rectify matters.

By no means do we ever hope to succeed in all of the above-listed maneuvers. That would not be a very practical approach, to say the least. If one or two offensive ploys can result in momentarily upsetting the opposition's defensive game plan and force him to concentrate more effort and attention on his defensive responsibility, we are satisfied in this respect.

MAN OFFENSIVE PATTERNS

In order for our offensive philosophy to remain in line with our defensive style of play, we have sought to combine certain power principles from several common continuity patterns. Corresponding with this idea of taking some of the more potent options from these basic offenses, we also seek to disguise our offensive movement by the use of an initial move or the same basic set for all the patterns —1:2:2—and break into the various offensive movements from this.

"Shuffle Series"

Our offensive mainstay versus the man-to-man defense is the elementary Shuffle series of blind-side picks and off-ball screens with the use of occasional pick-and-roll opportunities. Diagrams 9-1 through 9-4 show both the strong and weak-side moves which enable us to apply maximum pressure on the defense by posing a scoring threat from either side of the court with this perimeter continuity. Diagram 9-1 notes the basic Shuffle-cut (3 using the pick by 5 after the ball has been passed to the weak-side offensive player—1). Once 3 has cut off 5's pick, 5 rolls to the basket in anticipation of the pass from 1

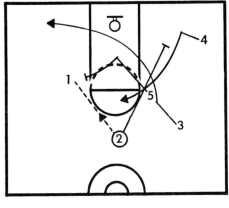

Diagram 9-1

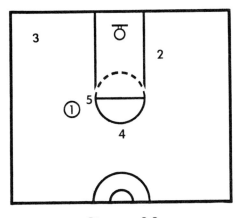

Diagram 9-2

for the short shot. 5 concludes his roll by coming to the high-post position on the opposite side of the key lane. As 3 cuts to the basket and looks for the assist pass from 1 for the easy lay-in, 2 moves low to set a screen for 4 to break to the foul line for the 15-foot jump shot. Diagram 9-2 illustrates the completed weak-side continuity rotation if 3 or 4 are not open. All positions are set in the same manner on the opposite side of the court once the rotation is complete. A pass from 1 to 4 can begin the rotation once again for another weak-side move if desired.

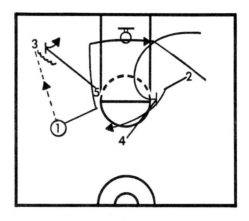

Diagram 9-3

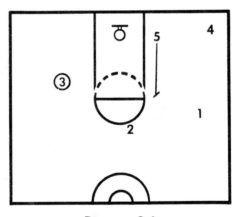

Diagram 9-4

Diagram 9-3 denotes the player movement when 1 passes to 3, thus initiating the strong-side option from the Shuffle set. Once again, we screen and cut away from the ball (4 and 2); however, we have added a pick-and-roll situation (5 and 3) on the ball. This is done with the assurance of floor balance if not successful. The pick-and-roll takes place prior to the off-ball screen-and-roll by 4 and 2. If 3 cannot score or successfully get the ball to either 5 or 4, 2 who is serving as the safety value, receives the outlet pass. Diagram 9-4 shows the completed rotation from the strong-side option and the maintenance of the Shuffle floor balance.

Two other Shuffle options we use are the Kentucky "Blind Pig" (Diagram 9-5) and the high-post "scissors" cut (Diagram 9-6). The "Blind Pig" is begun from the strong side, when 3 signals 1 to come to the high-post to receive the ball, while 2 attempts to shake his defender for the pass from 1 and the easy score. Whenever we employ the high-post split, or scissors, the player with the ball (either 2 or 3) hits the post and begins the split. The other player serves as the second cutter on the split. When the point (2) does not get the ball, he continues down the lane and sets a pick for 4, who then cuts to the basket, looking for a pass from 5 who has pivoted to a position facing the hoop.

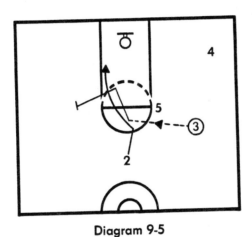

Diagram 9-5

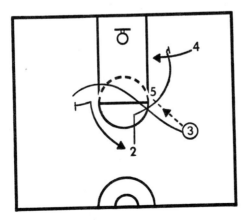

Diagram 9-6

"Double Stack"

This is another of the power offensive tactics we have used with success over the years when we have been fortunate enough to have a good one-on-one player who can also handle the ball. Employing a set of this nature can pose a serious problem to the coach who believes your team to be a strictly pattern continuity ball club. Diagram 9-7 depicts the initial Double Stack set with 2 and 3 representing our forwards, or two most aggressive offensive rebounders. Players 4 and 5 are our two better angle shooters aside from 1, who is allowed to shoot from both the angles as well as the point position. Ultimately, we prefer 1 to be able to work himself free for a couple of high-percentage 15-foot jump shots to start the game and thus commit the defense to focus their attention towards this offensive maneuver.

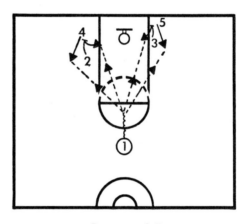

Diagram 9-7

As 1 makes his move to the basket, 2 and 3 pick for players 4 and 5, hoping to force the opponent to switch assignments and perhaps create a mismatch inside which we can possibly capitalize on. If the opponent does not perform a switch, either 4 or 5 will be open for a 12- to 15-foot shot. The lower four players will continue to pick for each other as needed while 1 remains back to assume the necessary safety position.

The Double Stack offense is designed as a "quick hitter" type of formation to open up the defense for the high-percentage field goal attempt. Since this offense has little continuity built in, we frequently use it as an initial move to get into either the Shuffle or 1-4 continuity patterns. It is a very effective ploy when used against a team that bases its defense around a man-to-man or 1:2:2 zone.

"Single Stack"

The Single Stack offense is merely a modification of the Double Stack. Whereas the Double Stack is primarily a perimeter attack, the Single Stack permits us to exploit the lower key area on whichever side of the court we feel we can create an advantageous situation. Note the player placement in Diagram 9-8 as compared with the Double Stack (Diagram 9-7)—only slight alterations have been made, thus making it relatively simple for the players to change in and out of the two stack formations. Unlike the Double Stack, this offense has a degree of continuity to it and thus we can adapt it to both weak and strong-side options. However, we will usually opt to go with the strong-side options on two out of three occasions since this pattern offers much better interior penetration of the opponent's defense. This particular pattern embodies the pick-and-roll on the ball (2 screening for 1) and also away from the ball (4 screening for 5).

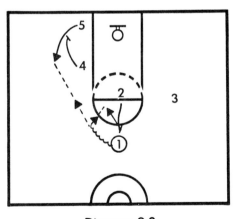

Diagram 9-8

1's initial responsibility is to use the pick by 2 to set up his man and drive to the strong side of the floor, looking for 2's roll to the foul line. If 2 is not open, which will be the case against most zones, he will perform an interchange with 3, who then becomes the deep safety. As this is taking place, 2 positions himself to be able to crash the offensive boards once the shot is taken. 4 screens for 5 to get open and receive the penetrating pass from 1. Once 5 receives the ball, he immediately looks for the 15-foot shot and if this is not available, waits for player 4 to set a screen on his man for the pick-and-roll to develop. While this is going on, 1 continues to remain wide—free-throw line extended—to serve as the safety should a pattern reversal be necessary.

Diagram 9-9 illustrates the high-post rub from the weak-side option off the Single Stack. Here, 1 passes to 3 and runs a cut off 2's pick. Should he not get a quick return pass from 3, he continues around the double screen set by players 4 and 5. Player 3 now has the option for a free-lance move of his own to the basket or a reversal pass back to 2, who, in turn, looks inside to player 5, coming off 4's pick or to 1 for the baseline jump shot.

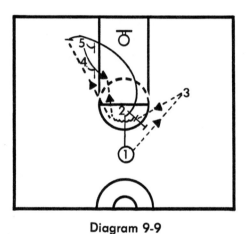

Diagram 9-9

"1-4 Options"

Because of the interior movement and numerous clearout opportunities, this continuity offense is one of the most popular in the game today. The clearout option we use is simply diagrammed in 9-10. Player 1 signals for either 2 or 3 to clear to the opposite side of the floor and remain low. As this outside man vacates his original position, the inside player on the cleared side—player 5 in this instance—steps up to set the screen for 1's drive to the goal. If 1 is unable to penetrate or use

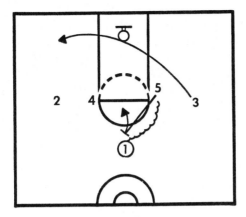

Diagram 9-10

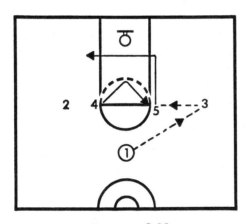

Diagram 9-11

the pick-and-roll as it unfolds, and is forced to terminate his dribble, we can easily reverse the ball back to 5 and begin running any of the other 1-4 or Shuffle options to either the weak or strong side of the floor. This inclusion of one offense within another is one of the many new trends in the continuity school of offensive theory brought about by the prominent coach at North Carolina, Dean Smith. There is no question of the degree of success that Coach Smith has enjoyed over the last few years, and part of this must go to his offensive ingenuity.

Diagram 9-11 refers to the 1-4 penetration by our "big" men once the ball is brought into the front court. If it is apparent that we are much quicker up front than our opponent, we will attempt to get the ball inside in this manner and establish a one-on-one opportunity. When this maneuver does not provide the desired opening, a simple reversal will again set our 1-4 continuity in motion. We will also resort to an outside move from the 1-4 which will be discussed later under the zone options (see Diagram 9-18). When run with the reversal, this pattern will work well against a majority of the tight man defenses as well as the sagging variations.

"Hi-Low Passing Game"

Against both the tight and sagging man defenses, we attempt to display a variety of offensive sets with numerous options that can direct the goal attack by our better players. Certain player skills will always be nullified by some teams and it thus becomes imperative for us to shift to another offensive maneuver or other players to get the high-percentage 15-foot shot. Both the above criteria can be met by the employment of another popular continuity pattern—the Hi-Low Passing Game, used so successfully during the past several seasons by U.S.C. coach, Bob Boyd.

The "quick hitters" such as the Double Stack and the 1-4 Clearout do not always provide enough overall movement to produce good shot selection. Passing Game patterns can serve to provide both the quick shot and the assurance of continuity should the opening not avail itself after the first two or three passes. When you are behind, or in a type of catch-up game, this is an excellent weapon to have at your disposal. This will also speed up the tempo of the game if that is your intent.

This offensive tactic is perhaps one of the most frequently discussed topics at the major clinics held around the country. Coaches are always fascinated by this form of ruled, "free-lance" style of play. It is undoubtedly the best means of making sure that your best offensive players take the majority of shots. The execution of the Passing Game is a thing of beauty to watch. However, it is my opinion that unless your lower-level programs teach Passing Game theory, you will have a difficult time successfully installing it at the high school level. Junior college and college players are naturally much more talented and able to adapt easily to this style of play. The high school coach installing this offense will find that his major problem will be keeping the players away from the ball in constant motion. Younger players have a tendency to stand around when either not about to receive a pass or otherwise be directly involved in the ball flow. Therefore, one of the options we have incorporated in the Passing Game involves the motion of the men opposite the ball.

Rules for the Passing Game are as simple or complex as the coach wants to make them. Our rules follow in the same vein as the other offenses we use: with a majority of picks away from the ball.[1] Simply stated, these rules consist of:

1. Positioning of players in a 1:3:1 set with two inside players—one on the foul line and the other on the baseline—and the three better perimeter shooters outside the key area.

2. Play is begun by an initial pass and screen away from the pass by one of the perimeter players. Ideally, this pass should be made on the side opposite the low-post (Diagram 9-12). The player receiving the screen comes toward the ball, while the player with the ball looks for a quick one-on-one move to the basket.

3. High-low post play consists basically of a series of interchanges with motion directed toward the position of the ball. Diagram 9-13 depicts this interchange movement as player 3 passes into the post (who is then free to go to the basket) and continues to screen away from the ball.

In Diagram 9-13, note that player 1 is not directly involved in the screening or passing process and it is here that many of the younger players fail to react instinctively or intelligently to off-ball play. When this situation presents itself, we insist that he use the low post to set his man up for a potential blind-side cut to the ball (Diagram 9-14) should player 5 not be able to maneuver for an open shot. As in all offensive patterns, timing is of the upmost importance and when correctly executed, the players using this off-ball pick will find themselves in an ideal scoring position if the post is able to get them the ball.

---

[1]Many teams run the Passing Game by screening on the ball following the pass. Regardless of the screening direction taken, the most important point to note concerning this offense is that your team is able to set strong and effective screens and execute the roll to the basket.

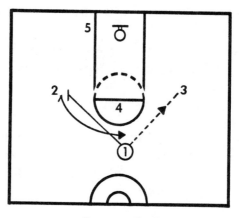

Diagram 9-12

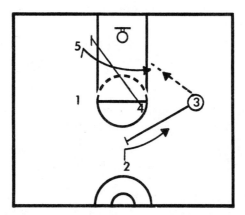

Diagram 9-13

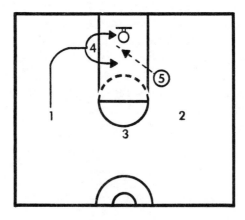

Diagram 9-14

ZONE OPTIONS

In order to prevent the opposition from starting play with a direct match-up defense, we take great care in teaching our floor captain to split their initial zone front. Thus, when confronting any of the even-front zones, we rely essentially on the following offenses as the basis for our attack:

1-4: Inside and Outside moves with Reverse Action Shuffle

Stack: Usually the Single variation

Hi-Low Passing Game

Odd-Frontal Gap

Against the one-man, or odd-front zones, we concentrate our attack in the following sets listed below:

Double-front Stack

Shuffle

2:1:2 Passing Game

Even-Frontal Gap

Since our players are relatively familiar with the above-mentioned offensive formations when coping with varying degrees of man-to-man pressure, we attempt to maintain the same basic sets when confronted by the numerous zone defenses. The zone options differ only slightly from the man patterns. For example, free-lance drives to the basket are replaced by individual moves to set up another player for the high-percentage field goal attempt. We continue to employ an endless amount of screens on the opponent—both on and away from the ball. Offensive movement continues as dictated by the continuity pattern with one major exception: instead of moving from floor position to floor position, *we now shift from zone seam to zone seam in accordance with continuity floor position.*

"Shuffle Zone Options"

Two specific Shuffle zone patterns which provide the desired high-percentage shot are illustrated in the following set of diagrams (9-15 through 9-17). All zones are taught to shift with the ball, therefore, one of our most successful, though unorthodox, patterns capitalizes on this very element. Diagram 9-15 demonstrates one such weak-side option when player 4 is our best perimeter shooter and we want him to take the majority of our shots. This amounts to a simple pass-over pattern. Once the initial pass from player 2 to 1 is made, 5 and 3 screen the defenders in their vicinity and thus the opposite side of the floor is practically open for player 4 to put up an uncontested shot at the goal. After this option has been run several times, though not necessarily in succession, the zone will attempt to fight through the screens or cheat on them completely, at which time player 1 is free to pass inside to either 3 or 5 for a good-percentage shot. If nothing transpires, he can signal for the floor to balance itself on the opposite side of the court and run another weak-side or strong-side move (Diagram 9-16).

The strong-side Shuffle zone option is essentially the same as the man option without the pick-and-roll on the ball. Here, (Diagram 9-17) we look to penetrate the zone interior by flooding certain seam areas—movement by 3 and 5, while presenting a blind-side screen by the point (2), who then rolls through the middle once 4 commences his dribble out of the corner. Once again, floor balance is achieved by player rotation to the same position as in the man attack on the opposite side of the court.

By meshing these two zone options together, they can: (1) provide good shot selection; (2) keep the floor spread and well-balanced; (3) overload specific areas and force the zone to shift constantly. This is ideally what we look for in all our zone offensive continuity patterns.

"1-4 Zone Patterns"

As previously noted, both the 1-4 options we use against the two-front zones can also be effectively employed against a man defense. These are primarily used against the two and three-man front zones, however, they can also be effective against the 1:3:1 zone match-ups. For lack of better terminology, we refer to these moves as the Inside and Outside, just as we do with the man options. Both have excellent reverse-action movement and it is from here that we expect to get a majority of our scoring.

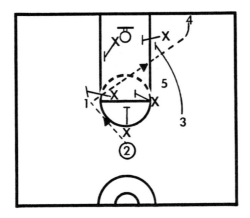

Diagram 9-15

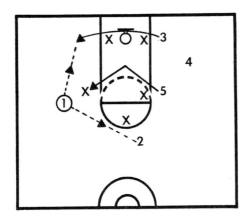

Diagram 9-16

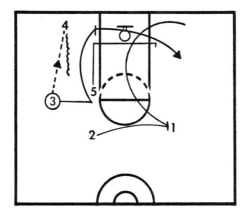

Diagram 9-17

Diagram 9-18 shows the beginning of the Outside option once player 3 receives the ball from the point (1). He has the choice of passing to either player 4 or 5, breaking to the high- and low-post areas. If neither is open, 3 reverses the ball back to 1, who then drives off the pick set for him by player 2 on the high defender (see Diagram 9-19). As player 1 drives past X_1, 5 shifts to the ball-side of the baseline. X_3 must now commit himself to either 1's drive or 5's baseline activity. Should he decide to confront 1, player 5 will be open for a short shot on the baseline. On the other hand, if X_3 decides to remain low, 1 will have the open shot. Player 4 will roll down the

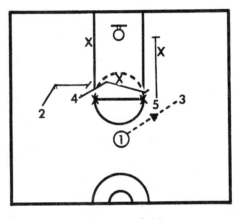

Diagram 9-18

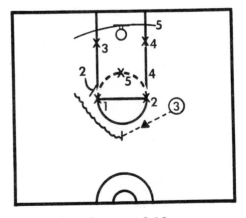

Diagram 9-19

middle seam only if X_5 chooses to get into the action. After player 1 has used the pick by 2, 2 rolls to the top of the key to become the safety should 1 be prevented from penetrating. Thus, the rotation is complete.

The Inside movement is the more difficult of the two to perform because of the problem of getting the ball inside on the initial pass. Because most good zone defensive teams emphasize covering the middle, they will be successful in denying the first penetrating pass. However, since the 1-4 is a strong continuity pattern, we usually will run either an initial move or an Outside move with a reversal and then counter with the Inside pattern. Diagram 9-20 shows the off-ball pene-

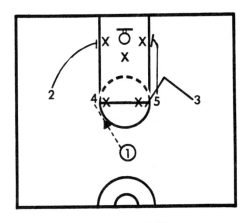

Diagram 9-20

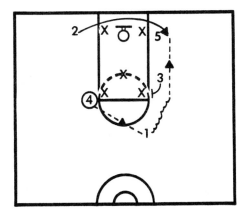

Diagram 9-21

tration by the offense once the inside pass has been made. As player 4 gets the ball he must pivot and face the basket, making his decision to attack the goal with a drive, pass low to a teammate, or pass back to 1 and begin reverse action. Illustrated in Diagram 9-21 is the reverse action and resulting baseline shot by player 2 off the pick set by 5 on the base defender. Note that once again, player 1 has the option of taking the shot as he drives off 3's screen or passing low. It should be clear by now that player 1 is our best outside shooter and also one of our better ballhandlers since he must work off so many picks with the ball.

"Stack Moves vs. the Zones"

Since the Stack is an area-attacking pattern, this is primarily used to penetrate the interior baseline segments of the zone defense. Its operation is very similar to that described for the man-to-man defenses.

As player 1 brings the ball across mid-court, he has the option of hitting 2 with a pass or using him as a screener to run a strong-side maneuver. Diagram 9-22 points out the options available when the high post (2) has the ball, while Diagram 9-23 depicts the over-load advantages provided by the strong-side pattern.

When facing a one-man front zone, we modify the stack slightly so as to pose a double front attack (Diagram 9-24). We attempt to force the defensive point man to declare on the offensive player on the weak side (2), who will then pass back to 1 and cut opposite his pass. 1 then is able to make the easy pass to either players 4 or 5, whoever is open.

"Gapping"

Although we do very little of this type of offensive maneuvering, it is necessary for us to possess this tool when we need a quick shot or a temporary variation in our offensive tactics. This can shake up your opponent if it appears that your offensive style of play is too slow or patterned. Our gapping theory merely amounts to placing men in the seams of the zone, with or without a post player, and having them drive and pass the ball until a good shot avails itself. In most cases, we use a single post and the two rules that guide our play in this respect are:

1. Post player sets up opposite the ball and roams toward

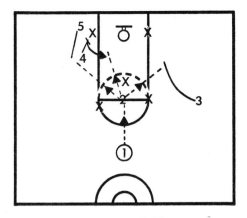

Diagram 9-22

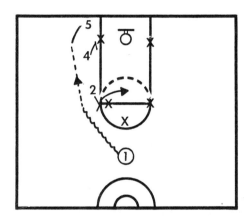

Diagram 9-23

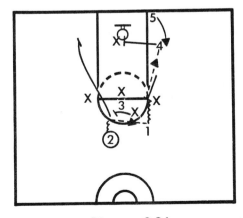

Diagram 9-24

the ball constantly in and around the seams of the zone defenders.

2. Player with the ball shoots if open or drives the ball into two zone defenders, and then looks to pass off to the open players for the shot.

"Passing Game Play"

The offensive fronts of the Passing Game can be easily altered to counter virtually any of the defensive fronts. The High-Low operation, which we noted earlier in the discussion against the man defenses, is essentially the same for the zone defenses with the lone exception that when screens are not possible to free players, they continue to move into the seams of the zone.

Our variation of the two-man front Passing Game operation is based upon the same fundamental principles as the High-Low series with a single post. Thus, we have incorporated the philosophy of gapping with the elements of the Passing Game when facing the stronger zone teams. Above all, this modification of the Passing Game is also an excellent quick-shot producer. Because of its overall flexibility, many coaches agree that both Passing Game patterns and modifications represent offensive basketball in its purest state.

WORKING THE OPPOSITION'S TOP PLAYERS

Since we are committed to maintain a harassing degree of pressure on the opponent's most skilled offensive performers when playing defense, we are dedicated to making them work as hard as possible while we have possession of the basketball. They must put out when defending us! A significant segment of our defensive game-plan theory is built around the very fact that many of today's top players make an all-out effort only at the offensive end of the court. Thus, the total effectiveness of these players will logically be reduced once they are obligated to deal with a demanding defensive assignment. Our method of attacking the opposition's better players while they are on defense revolves around two rather broad generalizations:

When faced with a zone defense, our primary attack
is directed toward the area of the opposition's better players.

Against the man defenses, we attempt to isolate certain players, thus creating possible one-on-one situations, pitting our best offensive players against their best offensive players.

Aside from physically draining the opposition's better player(s), as noted in the above rationale, we want to get our opponent into foul trouble so that his offensive aggressiveness is measurably diminished. When we face a team with only one superior performer, it is generally unusual for him to be guarding our best offensive player and, therefore, we must be patient enough to wait until such a one-on-one or overload situation presents itself. For example, after turning the Shuffle or Passing Game offenses over two or three times, the defense will have been forced to switch assignments several times and thus the designated opponent will be in a vulnerable position for one of our better players to test him. This "test" involves three specific items: (1) observing his particular defensive skills—can he do this or that . . .; (2) straining his conditioning factor—working him hard at both ends of the court; and (3) forcing him to assume a tough defensive task regardless of his particular foul situation.

Player exploitation is nothing new in the game of sport, and it serves as the ideal ploy for our style of combination defensive basketball. When an opposing player is involved in this form of play, it can become a most frustrating experience for both him and his coach. If correctly employed, this offensive methodology will present the opposing coach with a most perplexing dilemma: to remain with the same offensive and defensive tactics, or revise his strategy to relieve the pressure on his better players. This has proved to be a good tactical weapon in situations where we have been severely out-manned.

From a practical standpoint, this technique of working the opposing players at both ends of the court is relatively simple in theory, but takes constant practice to perfect. Basketball today is a physically demanding game of intense pressure. Therefore, by exploiting our opponent in this manner, we will be more physically capable of performing our game plan than he is of his. The longer we are able to continue this pace, the greater the possibility of neutralizing such a single dominant player.

CHAPTER 10

Carrying Out the
Combination Game Plan

In order to survive in today's fast-pace game, a team must possess the necessary skills to counter his opponent adequately as the game proceeds. In accordance with this "chess game" philosophy of coaching noted in several of the previous chapters, the combination team will be initially better able to meet the demands of this style of play. Constant countering takes a knowledgeable and versatile team, well-versed in fundamental team play. We have found that our better combination teams have also been our better "chess game" teams since they are familiar with adjusting and matching our play to the demands of the game; thus, our overall transitions have been much smoother in appearance. As a result, we have sought to capitalize on this element in as many ways as possible.

EARLY GAME ADVANTAGES

Combination defensive basketball, in conjunction with a multiplicity of offensive patterns, can go a long way to control the early tempo of the game. The earlier we can commit the opponent into making an adjustment the more successful, we believe, we are in our pre-game approach. This, of course, is purely psychological speculation on our part and can backfire unless approached with the proper perspective. We do not want our players to place any unnecessary pressure on themselves and become upset if this cannot be accomplished. Whenever it happens that the opposition is forced into a counter situation, our players can sense it and their play reflects an injection of confidence. During the first few minutes several indicators will tell whether or not we have established any early dominance or control:

1. The opponent calling the first time-out.
2. Getting a quick foul or two on the opposition's ''star'' player(s).
3. Dominating backboard play at both ends of the court.
4. Tactical revisions of the style of play.
5. Forcing three or four quick turnovers that result in scores.
6. Noticing that their top scorers handle the ball sparingly, or not at all.

The quick, aggressive nature of combination defensive play will serve to upset almost any pre-set offensive game plan the opponent might have. To our way of thinking, it is the latter two indicators in the list which are the most significant factors that we rely on our defense to control. The actual manner in which these are carried out depends to a large extent on the type of team we are playing—big rebounding team or a good shooting team, etc.

Once it is obvious that the opposing team will be forced to call a time-out to adjust to our defensive tactics, we will invariably make an adjustment oursevles to further keep them off-guard. For us, this is a rule of thumb and the players are prepared for it as the time-out is called. Our goal here is not to have them call another time-out to counter this move, but to further adjust their offensive attack until it leads to confusion among their players. This has been an effective weapon for us and its real beauty is that it is so simple to perform.

TIME-OUTS AND HALFTIME SITUATIONS

The time-out and its execution are almost as important as the basket scored from the offensive pattern! This phase of the game is perhaps one of the most valuable, yet mis-used, features of the game that we as coaches often neglect. The time-out can and must be fully utilized to your advantage! These breaks in play action afford sufficient time for numerous adjustments to be made. However, if any such adjustment is to be considered at this time, it must be carefully calculated in terms of its potential overall as well as that of its immediate effectiveness. It is my personal philosophy that whenever we call for a time-out, *no major team changes are to take place*—this includes all the hasty changes which we are so tempted to make.

With reference to the above note regarding major changes, it is my feeling that there is not enough time for strategic, all-encompassing alterations involving more than two players. The one minute you are allotted is not meant to be a substitute for the half-time talk. It was not designed for the purpose of being a mini-half time, and therefore we should not use it as such!

Your position as the head coach does not allow you to carefully analyze your offensive and defensive play, since you are busy observing the opposition's play. Therefore, during the game, the assistant coach records certain specifics of both teams, noting possible alternatives you might employ later on. The final decision, of course, lies with the head coach, but it is certainly a tremendous help if your assistant coach can provide an in-game analysis.

Throughout the years, I've seen a great many time-out situations botched, and was often guilty myself until I began to carefully observe the great college coaches in action during this interlude. Two facts came through loud and clear: (1) during the time-out, there must only be one person speaking—*you must dictate* and; (2) this must be done in a clam and re-assuring manner without any display of apprehension. Because of the time limit, there is no time for any other means of handling the time-out—at least successfully.

Basically, our purposes for calling a time-out are three fold:

1. Positioning of players as to their specific offensive or defensive assignments.

2. Pointing out weaknesses in the opponent which we can exploit.

3. Psychologically re-grouping team members when necessary.

Every time-out we take must be aimed at improving our play. We never use this time as a designated rest period. I believe, however, that we can accomplish both a short physical rest as well as taking steps to increase our effectiveness. Perhaps the one point we stress most during our called time-out is for the players not to hurry their play. This remains true even when we are behind. All players have a tendency to want to rush the attack in order to catch up and it has been my experience that whenever we have done so, we have fallen further and further behind.

It is also possible for the coach to tell when the opposition is about to take one of its time-outs. With the aid of the assistant coach's analysis, we can take advantage of the time-out taken by the opposing coach. As noted earlier, depending on the situation we may temporarily change the defense, based on the assumption that they have made the proper adjustment, *i.e.,* from a Diamond-and-One to a Box-and-One, or to a standard type zone—for the purpose of frustration.

Halftime

Regardless of the score at the intermission, our players realize that this is a most pivotal point in the game. Furthermore, they are aware that this will be looked upon as a planning session by the coaching staff—either for remaining in the lead (protection philosophy) or for catching up (revising tactics). The half-time interlude is merely an extended time-out in which much more team and individual attention can be dealt with. In this respect, we attempt to take full advantage.

Once the players' personal needs are taken care of, we gather around the chalkboard to review briefly what transpired during the first half, noting the strengths and weaknesses of our team effort. Although time allows for several detailed adjustments, we prefer to make only minor alterations while preparing the team for the possibility of more adjustments being made during the later stages of the second half of play. Most adjustments that we do enact during the halftime consist of individual positioning within the offensive and defensive framework.

Since this period of the game is to be a learning situation as well as one of rest, the coach should use discretion in his approach to game theory. In order to continue play successfully, a positive manner must be put forward. Players should never be chastised or ridiculed for their play. It is true that some players require more stimulation than others and respond to different stimuli, and if this is the case, they should be taken aside and dealt with individually. There is not sufficient time for yelling and screaming when a low-keyed, methodical approach can achieve the desired result and will help to unite the players for a good effort in the second half. Even during the heat of battle, it is sometimes hard to restrain ourselves; we must realize that our prime purpose during the half is to prepare the players to perform well after the intermission. Only in a low-pressure atmosphere can they both relax physically and concentrate mentally on the coach's directions.

Concluding the halftime talk is as important as the total of what has been said during the break. Depending on the rapport and overall relationship of the coach with his players, the manner in which the team takes the court will be determined. Much has been, and will continue to be, said concerning the emotional pitch players must reach upon taking the court following the half. However, I believe that if they have listened carefully to what has been discussed and then are given some form of positive reinforcement, they will be in the right frame of mind to play out the game.

IN-GAME PRESSURE VARIATION

As might be assumed, during the course of a game it is not unusual for us to alter our defensive strategy many times. By employing only minor changes in our defense, we may show as many as ten to 15 variations to keep the opponent at bay. This is true for our offensive attack also, although we definitely are much more flexible in our defensive approach to the game. Our basic rule regarding this facet of play is that whenever a particular defense is no longer functional, we will shift to one of the pre-planned alternatives, but we do not totally discard any defense for we may need to rely on it later in the game.

There are, of course, certain pivotal places in the game where coaches prefer to change their defense, whether or not the defense they are in is working well. This method of altering defenses works harmoniously with the combination style of defense superbly. Depending on the effectiveness of this change in defense, we will stay with it, return to the initial defense, or further alter the plan. We have four specific times when we will automatically change our defensive attack:

1. When the opposition calls for a time-out.

2. On a made foul shot.

3. At the quarter and half breaks.

4. Sometimes on a jump ball or break-away basket.

I say that this is automatic because our floor captain calls out the defensive switch and relays this to the players. This will come as no surprise to any of our players since they are usually given their individual assignments for two or three specific defenses prior to the start of the game. Very seldom has the defensive transition not been smooth—almost to the point of going undetected by the opposition.

We prefer to believe that after we have played a league opponent once, we must vary the defense the next time we face him. In most instances we use the combinations during most of the first game, and it is only good coaching philosophy to begin the next encounter with one of the standard zone match-ups or a straight man defense. Because of the problem of countering the combinations in the first game, the opponent undoubtedly has prepared for another game of facing this type of defense. This is not to say that we will remain with the standard defenses throughout the course of the game. In our pre-game talk we will give the players one standard defense and two combinations to switch in and out of at certain intervals and this is usually enough to keep the opponents guessing as to what we are doing on defense—especially when we add a press to accompany these.

RECOGNITION OF VICTORY

We are all aware of player superiority—simply being out-studded from the opening tip. These are long nights for both coaches and players, but they do happen from time to time and the only things that seemingly keep the team together during and following this type of ball game are the pride and confidence the players have in themselves. Aside from teaching and reinforcing fundamental basketball theory and putting it into practice on a team concept, the coach must be able to instill this confident pride whether his team is winning or losing. Although the psychology of coaching is another topic, the success of any coaching system must be measured by more than the won-lost record—the dedication to, and execution of, a specific idealogy. Such is the case for the combinations.

Whenever an individual player or group of players can place their fingers on the real reason why we won or lost a particular game, I believe that they have gained a great deal. The answer they most frequently give is that there was a breakdown in team execution. Seldom has any player pointed to another as the cause for defeat, yet they are quick to point to other teammates who kept us in the game. All coaches like to hear this from their players, and ours are pretty well conditioned to respond in this manner. From the first day of practice until the last game of the season they are constantly approached by the interworkings of offensive and defensive team play. I feel that this is one of the best ways for the players to learn the game and once they gain this attitude, they will be better ballplayers.

The combination defensive system delves deeper into the actual inner workings of team basketball than any other means of measurement. As the players increase their understanding of the various segments of this concept of the game, they are better able to execute both the indivudal and team offensive and defensive skills. This has proved especially true for those players who are directly involved with the majority of ''denial'' responsibilities. By the middle of the pre-season, all the players have had the opportunity to work a single-coverage situation. The most noticeable improvement in their immediate play is on offense—setting and using the screens more effectively than we had hitherto done along this line.

Evaluating the combination system is difficult and at best a vague task. By the time our players graduate and are ready for junior college or major college ball, it is my hope that they can easily make the transition to a higher caliber of play not just because of their natural ability, but also because of their understanding of the game. Even in our weaker seasons, we have had one or two players who have gone on to play college ball for that reason.

Team and individual defense wins games, and it also serves as the best teacher in the game today. The more thorough the defense—all encompassing in nature—the greater the potential of the team. It is for this reason that I believe combination defensive play is clearly one of the most progressive dimensions in the evolution of the game of basketball.

INDEX